THE OCEAN
IN ENGLISH HISTORY

THE OCEAN
IN ENGLISH HISTORY

BEING
THE FORD LECTURES

BY

JAMES A. WILLIAMSON

OXFORD
AT THE CLARENDON PRESS

Oxford University Press, Amen House, London E.C. 4

GLASGOW NEW YORK TORONTO MELBOURNE WELLINGTON
BOMBAY CALCUTTA MADRAS CAPE TOWN

Geoffrey Cumberlege, Publisher to the University

FIRST EDITION 1941
Reprinted photographically in Great Britain
at the University Press, Oxford, 1948
from sheets of the first edition

PREFACE

IN 1938 I was honoured by the invitation to deliver the Ford Lectures for 1939–40. They were prepared before the outbreak of war and were delivered in the summer of 1940, when no one can have been more conscious than the lecturer of the incongruity of discoursing on past history amid the shattering events of May and June.

Many of my obligations to the work of others are mentioned in the footnotes. Many are of long standing, spread over thirty years, and some have been derived not from books but from conversation. Such acquisitions lose their distinctness of origin and incorporate themselves in the thought of their borrower, so that it is hardly possible to specify them. They form, nevertheless, the substance of my stock-in-trade, for I confess that my own claims to originality of thought are small. More easy to acknowledge are debts of a different sort, and my gratitude is due to Professor F. M. Powicke, Sir Charles Grant Robertson, Mr. A. L. Rowse, and Mr. J. N. L. Baker for having done their best to set a stranger at his ease in the unaccustomed surroundings of an Oxford lecture theatre.

J. A. W.

CONTENTS

I

THE DISCOVERY OF AMERICA

THE purpose of these lectures is to outline the working of one of the many formative influences of modern England, from the opening of the Tudor period to the threshold of the nineteenth century. It is not easy to find a good name for this aspect of the national life, but, if we may use the word interest as it was used formerly in those widely known terms the Landed Interest and the Moneyed Interest, we may describe the subject as the Oceanic Interest.

It was a product of the medieval renaissance, and it originated, not in these islands, but among the Latin peoples of western and southern Europe. The beginnings of its contact with English life are discernible in the fifteenth century, when speculation about the possibilities of the unknown Atlantic began to find utterance. It was at first very limited, and even the discovery of America made but a small impression upon English consciousness until half a century after it had taken place. Then, in the second half of the Tudor period, the interest grew and became a national concern. It employed the thoughts and actions of many men, and soon it was producing wealth in new forms and influencing the policy of the state. English captains, financed by English merchants and patronized by the ministers of the Crown, began to traverse the Atlantic in growing numbers. Some, but not the majority, went in search of plunder; and that aspect of the movement has often received too great a prominence in the narration of Elizabethan history. Others looked for trade, new products for English consumption and new markets for the manufactures of English craftsmen.

B

Others again prospected for colonial sites in which the surplus population of England might find new homes. From the outset there were projectors who regarded the Atlantic, our nearest ocean, as a means to farther ends, and searched its four corners for passages leading to yet remoter regions of the world. Perhaps in that last word lies the clue to the novelty of the whole process. Before the discovery of America, England's external interests were European. After it they gradually became world-wide, although for a long time the chief scene of activity was the North Atlantic. For a hundred and fifty years after the death of Henry VIII not a decade passed without the origination of some new branch of gainful enterprise, or of some new colony or trading-post, upon the ocean which washes our own shores; until, by the Treaty of Utrecht, its main coasts and islands were dotted with British settlements, which yielded wealth to the parent country and drew their own life from her multitudes of ships.

During that early period the Atlantic for its own sake attracted our chief energies, but it had also an ulterior value. Besides being in itself a wealth-producing region it was the ante-chamber to another, the Indian Ocean and the Eastern seas beyond. To reach Asia was indeed the original, or almost the original, inspiration. It was long unfulfilled, for a century of effort was needed for Englishmen to reach the Far East. By the opening of the Stuart period they were there, and the Indian Ocean was added to the Atlantic as a scene of regular enterprise. Until the Restoration the Indian trade was precarious, but thenceforward it expanded rapidly. In the eighteenth century it extended to China, and the great ships poured into London the proceeds of a net-work of local trade-routes ramifying among all the lands and islands from the Persian Gulf to Canton.

The third ocean in the system of mercantile empire

was the Pacific, more commonly known in old colonial times as the South Sea. The English interest in the South Sea was not continuous. The Elizabethans began it, as they began most other enterprises, but after them there was a long interval. For a full hundred years, almost coinciding with the seventeenth century, scarcely an English ship sailed the waters of the greatest ocean, and hardly a thought was given to it by any English government as a likely field of enterprise. The eighteenth century did better. From Dampier to Cook a succession of British explorers played the leading part in revealing new lands and exploding ancient theories in the South Sea. After them came the whalers, the traders, and the colonists, to make it an area of modern British life as important as the Atlantic and the coasts of Asia.

The oceanic efforts of four centuries increased continuously in volume and effect. They proceeded from the energies of the English nation, and they reacted with important results upon its life. Projectors and propagandists brought opinion to bear upon governments. Doctrines, laws, and treaties became parts of the texture of public thought. Shipping in all its aspects became a leading national industry. Ambitious men looked for careers across the ocean. Tropical produce created new wants and new employments. The demand for export goods quickened the introduction of new methods into industry. And the fluid capital accumulated in the profitable trades of the tropics financed the mechanical revolution which changed the old rustic England into a nation of townsmen. Freedom of thought and action marched with the growth of all this energy; and humanitarianism and social improvement followed in freedom's wake. For good and for evil the England in which we live has sprung from many seeds, and not the least vital among them was set by the few daring men who first showed the way across the ocean in the fifteenth century.

It is natural, then, to begin this study with some considerations on the discovery of America, the discovery that has proved to be the watershed between medieval and modern life, and of the part that our own country played in it. The England of the fifteenth century was in many ways an alert and active country, and yet was very backward in curiosity about any regions of the world beyond those with which it had immediate contact. The area of its contacts was limited. Apart from the ecclesiastical connexion with Rome, it was in practice the area in which Englishmen were able to sell wool or woollen cloth. The wool trade took them to Spain and Portugal and the Biscay coast of France, but only irregularly through the Straits of Gibraltar to Italy and the Levant. It led them in large numbers to the Netherlands, and in smaller numbers to the Baltic and Scandinavia; and, coupled with the attraction of the northern fishery, it carried them every year to Iceland, which provided the longest open-water voyage regularly frequented by English shipping. English woollens went farther than their producers. Venetians, Florentines, and papal agents from Rome shipped wool to Italy as raw material for a superfine cloth manufacture, and brought to England choice Italian wares and the spices obtained from Arabs in the Levant. Both the profits and the world-knowledge accruing from the spice trade remained with its Italian monopolists. Similarly in the North, the Germans of the Hanseatic League distributed English cloth through central and eastern Europe and even into Russia, but were fairly successful in excluding Englishmen themselves from access to anything beyond the coastline of the continent. Geographical knowledge shared the limitations of the flag. Englishmen knew little of the Levant, and nothing of Russia and the countries that lay beyond. In former times English crusaders and pilgrims had known the Holy Land and its Asiatic neighbours. Now the Crusades had ceased, and few pilgrims went farther than Rome or St. James of Compostella. A ballad of the fifteenth century describes the voyage to 'Saint Jamys' as the ordinary pilgrim excursion. Chaucer had evidently heard of knightly adventurers to Lithuania and Russia, but their merchant successors a hundred years later had difficulty in maintaining a foothold in the Hanse ports of Lübeck and Danzig, and were excluded from the interior.

Not only were English travellers and seafarers limited in the scope of their activities, but English scholars in the fifteenth century paid little attention to the new information and the new speculations on distant geography which were developing on the continent. In this matter there was not only a halt but a regression. Even Saxon England had been interested in remote regions. Roger Bacon in the thirteenth century had been a geographer as well as a distinguished scholar in other sciences. In the fourteenth century it was at least plausible for the fabricator of the travels of Sir John Mandeville to attribute the work to an English writer; while somewhat earlier a quite genuine *Treatise of the Sphere* had been compiled by an Englishman, John of Holywood. It was so well regarded as a standard textbook that its popularity continued into the age of printing; no less than twenty-five editions of it are on record before 1500.[1] But all of these printed versions were continental, not English, and Holywood's name was rendered as Sacrobosco; so that the circulation of his book is no testimony to an English interest in such matters in the fifteenth century.

[1] G. H. T. Kimble, *Geography in the Middle Ages*, London, 1938, p. 80.

Nevertheless the geographical science in which England had for a time lost interest was but waiting to influence her destinies, and its leading ideas demand our attention.

Instructed geographers believed the earth to be a sphere, floating motionless and surrounded by revolving heavens. They realized that the earth's climates were arranged in zones of decreasing warmth from the equator to the poles; and until the fourteenth century most of them believed that the equatorial torrid zone was too intensely hot for human life to exist in it. The southern temperate regions were thus cut off from the northern by an impassable belt; and for this reason alone, and not from any notion that the earth was flat, it was heresy to assert the existence of antipodean peoples, since to do so would deny the Biblical teaching that all men are the sons of Adam. The inhabited parts of the world were therefore north of the equator, and it was universally believed that they consisted of the three continents of Europe, Asia, and Africa, with only small islands in addition.

A complete refutation of this limitation of the habitable world should have come from the travels of Marco Polo, who went by land to China in the late thirteenth century, and returned in Chinese shipping through the Straits of Malacca to the Indian Ocean and the Persian Gulf. By so doing the Venetian sailed thousands of miles in the tropics and was actually beneath the equator. But Marco's book had little immediate effect. It came too late for appreciation by such a giant as Roger Bacon, who would have perceived its significance. It was unjustly disbelieved by many of its early readers. Its author, moreover, lacked the academic learning even of his own period, so that he failed to fit his mighty discoveries into the accepted framework of the climatic zones. He gives no latitudes, few bearings (he had no compass), and few distances that are even approximately correct. Although he had seen infinitely more of Asia than had any previous European, it would not be possible to construct a map of the continent from his observations alone.

Only in the course of the fourteenth century did the knowledge gained by him and by later travellers slowly discredit the doctrine of the prohibitive heat of the tropic zone. In the fifteenth it was completely shattered by the voyages of Portuguese seamen on the west coast of Africa. But otherwise the old conception prevailed. The northern world was tripartite, consisting only of the three contiguous continents; and it followed that a westward voyage from Europe would lead to the eastern coast of Asia. Although the possibility had been known to the writers of ancient Rome, and was revived by the scholars of the Renaissance, it was late in the fifteenth century before it reached the stage of experiment.

Meanwhile there was another call to Atlantic enterprise in numerous legends asserting the existence of islands at less or greater distances from Europe. One such was the Island of the Seven Cities, colonized by Spanish refugees from the Saracen invasion of the eighth century. On late medieval maps this island frequently bears the name of Antilia; and when Marco Polo's book secured recognition, which it was very slow to do, as a valid description of the Far East, his account of Cipango or Japan was sometimes applied to the legendary Antilia, and the two tended to become identical in the geography of the Renaissance. Another supposed Atlantic island was that of Brazil, often located not far west of Ireland. It was named from its alleged profusion in brazil wood, a dyestuff already obtained under that name from the tropics of the Old World. Yet another group were the Islands of St. Brandan, discovered and settled by an Irish saint of antiquity, and since lost to view. These legends were current in all the western ports of Europe, and in the earliest stage of Atlantic discovery they were more potent stimulants to action than the scholarly speculation of the possibility of a western passage to Asia. For the legends had a basis of fact, in the existence of the Canaries, Madeira, and the Azores; and when those groups were successively discovered, the legends did not rest upon them, but took wing to yet farther islands still awaiting conquest in the mysterious West. New assertions continually reinforced the old stories. The belief in St. Brandan's was extraordinarily tenacious: as late as the reign of Charles I we find an Englishman petitioning for licence to discover and possess them.[1] Professional seamen were convinced by various signs that there was land not far beyond Ireland, where Brazil was said to lie. A Portuguese crew asserted that they had actually been in Antilia, where the sea-sand contained grains of gold, but the inhabitants were so sinister that nothing would induce the discoverers to revisit them.

The mystery of the Atlantic called with increasing urgency to a generation of seamen whose equipment hardly kept pace with their ambitions. Their ships were small, yet so heavy to work as to require excessively large crews. Gear was clumsier and of poorer quality than in later times. There was little knowledge of food preservation, and in this respect a long voyage involved perils that are scarcely realizable to-day, and a huge mortality was common. The magnetic compass had long been in use, and already it was known that the needle did not in all regions point to the polar axis of the heavens. For observing latitudes the navigator had his astrolabe with which to take the elevation of the pole star, a method which became inadmissible as one

---

[1] *Calendar of Colonial State Papers, America and W.I., 1574–1660*, pp. 128–9.

approached the equator. The Portuguese, on reaching the West African tropics, sought to obtain latitude by the sun, but accuracy had to await the work of Abraham Zacuto, a Jewish mathematician, who prepared tables of the sun's declination; and it was some time before these aids became available to seamen in general. Columbus, although he had made voyages with the Portuguese, alludes in his journal of 1492 to no other method of finding latitude than by the pole star. For longitude there was no guide whatever, save an estimate of the distance run from the last land whose position was known.

Many geographers of the fifteenth century made world-maps and globes showing the three continents, and by this time they were not afraid to extend the habitable areas beyond the equator. The fifteenth-century world-map was based upon that of Ptolemy, the Alexandrian geographer of the second century, whose work was fully rediscovered by Renaissance scholarship in the decade between 1410 and 1420. Ptolemy had made no attempt to draw the eastern coast of Asia, but it was supplied by guesswork fitted to the written descriptions of medieval travellers. This east coast of Asia was important to explorers, since by the tripartite theory it was the coast facing Europe across the Atlantic. It received a standardized form, in which it was given a great promontory just north of the tropic of Cancer, while the large island of Cipango was shown between that tropic and the equator, surrounded by a vast number of lesser islands fringing the continent in what Marco Polo had described as the Sea of Chin. To eastern Asia in temperate latitudes the name Cathay was generally applied, while its tropical region was called Manji.

Broadly speaking, we may say that there were two schools of geographical advance in the fifteenth century.

One was academic in its method and studied the records of the past, collating the classical authorities with the reports of medieval travellers, and using the mathematical work of Ptolemy in the measurement of the globe and the fixing of positions. Ptolemy's mathematical results had long been known, for they had been preserved by Saracen scholars and early communicated to the West. Ptolemy's maps, on the other hand, had been lost to sight for many centuries, and the rediscovery of his atlas about 1410 was a powerful stimulus to the academic thinkers. From their work proceeded the clarification of ideas on the distribution of the world's land-masses, and an increasing familiarity with the project of crossing the Atlantic as a means of approach to Cipango and Cathay. The academic school was most prominent in central Europe, and ultimately in Italy, where its ideas were at length enabled to bear fruit after they had made contact with the minds of sea-going men like Columbus and Cabot.

The habitat of the other school was in the seaports of western Europe, and especially of Portugal. Here, under the inspiration of Henry the Navigator, although learning was by no means neglected, the advance was by practical experiment, by successive voyages along the African coast and successive probings for Atlantic islands. The Canaries were already known, and there is some evidence that Madeira and the Azores had been visited and forgotten. During Henry's time all these islands were explored and occupied, and Africa charted to within a few degrees of the equator. But Portuguese thought, unlike that of Italy, did not take long leaps. It regarded the western Atlantic, not as a road to Cathay, but as promising further island discoveries, to be reached by extending the chain of stepping-stones from the known to the unknown. There is no clear evidence even that the project of reaching the Indian Ocean by rounding Africa took shape until some time after Prince Henry's death. From about 1480 the plan is apparent, but by that time the interest of all Christendom was growing, intercourse between scholars and seamen was closer, and the academic and the practical were about to join forces.

The place of England in these enterprises was at first insignificant. In the thirteenth century she had produced Roger Bacon. But the heritage of his work fell to Christendom as a whole, and England displayed no special fruits of his teaching. In one sense, however, the English friar was an ancestor of the great explorers of the Renaissance. The passages in his *Opus Majus* which treated of the westward passage round the sphere to Asia were closely copied by Cardinal Pierre d'Ailly in his fifteenth-century *Imago Mundi* ; and the *Imago Mundi*, which was printed before 1490 after a popular career in manuscript, was more than any other single work the authority that inspired the trans-Atlantic voyagers. Columbus, in reading and re-reading his copy, and enriching it with scribbled marginalia, was deriving instruction from a great English intellect. But this was exceptional, and it is true to say that in the formative fifteenth century England was backward, and indeed produced not a single man of any demonstrable influence in the academic progress of geography.

On the practical side there is a little more to be said, and it might be a great deal more if only evidence had survived; but the late fifteenth century is unhappily one of the badly recorded periods in our history. By making the most of what we have, by piecing together hints from this source and that, and cementing them by some probable but unproved conjectures, we may reach a provisional understanding of what took place.

All the information points to Bristol as the seat of

enterprise for the discovery of unknown land in the Atlantic; and there were reasons why Bristol should take the lead. Her seamen and merchants went regularly to Iceland in the fifteenth century to obtain supplies of salt fish, a traffic which accounts for many entries in the Bristol customs ledgers. English merchants in Iceland were in a position to hear of lands across the Atlantic whose existence was unknown to Europeans in general; for the sagas which record the ancient Norse discoveries of Greenland, Markland, and Wineland the Good were still living knowledge in Iceland. Of three principal sagas which narrate the deeds of Leif Erikson and his comrades there still exist transcripts that were made in Iceland in the fourteenth and early fifteenth centuries. An Icelandic geography of the same period names the western lands and describes their positions. A record of 1347 mentions the arrival of a ship from Markland.[1] And we have fifteenth-century maps of northern origin which show Greenland, although none has yet been discovered with delineations of the countries farther to the west. These facts are sufficient to show that the tenth-century discovery of America was living knowledge in fifteenth-century Iceland. It is reasonable to suppose that the Bristol men may have heard of it.

Bristol had also a contact to the southward with other men who had ideas on the unknown Atlantic. Her customs records show that Portuguese and Spanish ships came regularly into the port and that Bristol men had a large trade with Portugal. They show, moreover, that Bristol merchants were certainly taking cargoes to Madeira by 1480, and possibly also to the Azores; and that Azorean captains from that far colonial outpost were bringing their ships into Bristol. The association

[1] For a good short treatment of this subject see G. M. Gathorne-Hardy, *The Norse Discoverers of America*, Oxford, 1921.

of Bristol with the Portuguese navigators of the Atlantic is thus established.

Whether the inspiration was mainly from the north or from the south, it moved the men of Bristol to make voyages in search of Atlantic islands some time before the great Columbian age of discovery set in. In the summer of 1480 John Jay, a merchant who traded with both Iceland and Portugal, sent an eighty-ton ship to 'traverse the seas' to the west of Ireland in quest of the Island of Brazil. The commander was John Lloyd, one of the foremost sea-captains of Bristol. He failed to find the island, and returned to port in September after a stormy voyage. In the next year there was another expedition by two small vessels for the same purpose of locating the Isle of Brazil, and on this occasion the documents show that each ship carried a quantity of salt as part of her necessary stores.[1] Many years later, in 1498, a Spanish ambassador reported that 'for the last seven years the people of Bristol have sent out every year two, three, or four caravels, in search of the Island of Brazil and the Seven Cities'. From these scanty notices, preserved by chance when much other evidence has perished, we gain the impression of a fairly continuous series of Bristol voyages into the open Atlantic.

The belief in the existence of an unknown land in this direction was very persistent. As late as 1518 the Spanish geographer Enciso wrote that Brazil lay in 51 degrees of latitude and seventy leagues to the west of Ireland. We know that such a land does not exist. But near that position there is something that may well account for the sustained interest of the Bristol men, and which may even be the basis of the island legend. In 54 degrees of latitude, and about 100 miles from the Irish coast, the deep soundings of the ocean give place

[1] D. B. Quinn, 'Edward IV and Exploration', *Mariner's Mirror*, July, 1935.

to a comparatively shallow area. It is the Porcupine Bank, to-day a recognized fishing-ground for trawlers out of the Bristol Channel.[1] The discovery of this bank, or perhaps a long-standing knowledge of it, may account for the lading of salt in the mysterious voyage of 1481; for a cargo of fish might have paid the expenses of exploration. It may account also for the persistent belief in the island, since shallow soundings are commonly found near land. Whether the Bristol men found the Porcupine Bank is a conjecture. It is even possible that it was known many centuries before their time; for there is now in a Cardiff museum a fragment of Roman earthenware fetched up a few years ago in the net of a trawler on the Porcupine Bank.[2] Such a find sets the imagination working on the lost secrets of Atlantic history.

In 1492–3 the academic doctrines, by that time characteristic of Italy, and based upon broad considerations of the shape of the earth and its continents, suddenly bore fruit. Columbus sailed across the Atlantic and returned to announce that he had been in Asia, an astonishing piece of news to a generation which had watched the Portuguese reaching no farther than South Africa after many years and many voyages. With a well-found expedition Columbus, it seemed, had achieved at the first attempt the age-old project of reaching the East by way of the West. He had been in Hispaniola, which he identified with Cipango, and had coasted part of Cuba, which he took to be the great promontory of the main continent laid down on the academic maps.

[1] The Admiralty Chart shows the Porcupine Bank as an area whose centre is approximately in 54° N. and about 2° W. of the nearest part of Ireland. The soundings on the bank are from 82 to 95 fathoms, the depths between the bank and the Irish coast being about twice as much. The soundings on the great bank of Newfoundland are about 35–50 fathoms.   [2] *Journal of Roman Studies*, vol. xxiv, p. 220, no. 8 (1934).

The news aroused interest in England; and in England also Columbus had a counterpart named John Cabot, or Zuan. Cabota, like himself a Genoese by birth, but a naturalized citizen of Venice. Historical luck, the chance survival of evidence, has treated Columbus well and Cabot badly. If Columbus had died on his second voyage, and if his son and his friends had not been careful to preserve the record of his deeds, he would not rank as the great figure we know. The sorrows and clamours of his later years, the filial piety of Fernando Columbus, and the loyalty of Bishop Las Casas, not least in preserving that fascinating journal of his pioneer voyage, have made his personality and his record live. John Cabot lacked all these aids to remembrance. He seems to have died with his work but just begun; no contemporary historian wrote more than a paragraph about him; his son Sebastian, intent on his own career, scarcely ever mentioned his name. Yet it is possible that Cabot was a greater man than Columbus, his equal in originality and determination, his superior in knowledge and judgement. 'It is possible' is all that can be said. A little evidence remains, and fate has destroyed the rest.

Cabot came to Bristol about 1490, and he introduced to that enterprising seaport the things it most lacked, the Mediterranean ideas on world-wide commerce and the Renaissance teachings on the possibilities of the Atlantic, which reduced the search for mere islands to the status of a minor enterprise. It is fairly clear that Cabot had developed his plans before the success of Columbus was known, and that he was an originator and not an imitator of Columbus. He brought with him to England a knowledge of the oriental spice-trade, in which he had personally taken part in his Venetian days, by way of Egypt and the Red Sea. He brought also a skill in maps and globes and a wide reading in

Renaissance geography. Cardinal d'Ailly had taught him how to sail to Asia, and Marco Polo had shown him what to expect when he arrived there. His choice of Bristol was almost certainly an essential part of his plan, for it was not a place in which ordinary Italian traders did any business; their regular traffic was concentrated in London and Southampton. But Cabot had not come to England to engage in established trades. He was here to create a new one. The Bristol men had proved their zest for discovery, and he speedily made them ambitious to supplant Southampton as the head-quarters of the spice import. It may be asked why he brought his project to England at all. It was probably the only choice available. Venice would certainly have countenanced no competition with her ancient spice-trade through the Levant, and we know that at some date Cabot had already sought patronage in Portugal and Spain without success.

The merchants of Bristol became the allies of John Cabot. They could supply shipping and crews. He was poor and unable to finance his project, but he knew Cathay from Marco Polo's book, and he knew how to buy spices from personal experience. It is probable that his ideas on Asiatic trade were new to his Bristol friends, for there is no evidence that any man in England had yet studied the geographical literature that was exercising so many minds in southern Europe. They on their side had something to tell him, namely, the Icelandic knowledge that a main continent existed at no impossible distance across the North Atlantic. The Icelanders, so far as we know their writings, never suggested that their Wineland and Markland were parts of Asia, and neither, in all probability, did such a thing occur to the Bristol men. But it must have seemed obvious to Cabot, with the academic world-map in his mind. The tripartite world held only three

continents; and to the geographer all fell into order.
The northern parts of Europe were poor and bleak.
Those of Cathay would be of like nature, and, by the
Norse accounts, were peopled with intractable savages.
But they were continuous with Marco Polo's Empire of
the Great Khan to the southward, a land of civilization
and rich trade.

So the plan evolved, influenced by the news from
Spain. Columbus claimed to have reached Cipango
and Cathay. But a well-read man might doubt it, as
many did; for he had found neither spices nor civilized
Asiatics. Cabot's view was that Columbus had not
been far enough, and had stopped at islands in mid-
ocean. By Cabot's reckoning the nearest part of Cathay
was in the latitudes of the British Isles, and from that
point the continent slanted away south-westwards to
the tropics well beyond the islands discovered by the
Spaniards. He proposed to find the main continent
at its nearest point and thence to follow its coast to the
tropical regions, which he would thus attain without
trespassing on the Spanish discoveries.

The record, meagre though it is, sufficiently shows
that Henry VII took a keen personal interest in the project. In March 1496 he issued letters patent, conferring
upon Cabot and his deputies the monopoly of trade in
all the new lands they might discover in the King's
name, and conferring upon Bristol the right of being
the only port from which the new trade should be conducted. Spain heard of it, and her ambassador was
instructed to protest, but the undertaking went forward.

In 1497 the first English ship crossed the Atlantic, the
Matthew of Bristol. John Cabot commanded her, and
some merchants of Bristol went with him. After six
weeks' sailing they discovered a coast whose identity is
disputed with great vigour to the present day. Cabot's
journal, unlike that of Columbus, has not been pre-

served, and the evidence of the landfall is so vague that there can be no certainty on the matter; but the indications seem to point rather to Nova Scotia than to Newfoundland. Cabot followed the coast far enough to be able to claim it as a continent and not a small island, and then turned back. On his homeward course he may have sighted the outlying capes of Newfoundland. He certainly did find the shallow soundings of the great bank, and his Bristol mariners caught cod in such profusion that they declared it to be a better fishing-ground than the coast of Iceland.

Cabot came to London and reported to the King. He had no doubt of the nature of his discovery, and asserted that it was the mainland of Asia, 'the territory of the Grand Khan'. He was alluding, of course, to Marco Polo's Khan of Cathay, not knowing that the Mongol Empire had ceased to exist. This first voyage had been purely for discovery, and he regarded the discovery as made. Next time he would go with a trading fleet and follow the coast to tropical latitudes. There he would trade in spices, and over against the continent would find the rich island of Cipango replenished with gold and pearls. All this, he said, lay well beyond the discoveries of the Spaniards, and he showed maps and a globe to that effect. Spain's ambassador examined the maps and declared them to be false. Cabot's continent, he claimed, was already in the possession of his sovereigns. He was probably repeating the assertion of Columbus, that Cuba was a promontory of Cathay.

Henry VII disallowed the protest, and the enthusiasm of London rivalled that of Bristol. The King provided a large ship, and the Londoners found her cargo. At Bristol she joined four others laden by the merchants of that port, and Cabot sailed in command of all in 1498. What followed we do not know, save that a passage in a recently examined manuscript of the con-

temporary historian, Polydore Vergil, says that Cabot
and his ship disappeared, missing with all hands.[1] The
statement is positive enough, but it is not yet clear that
complete confidence can be placed in it. However, it
relates only to John Cabot and his ship, and does not
prove that the rest of the expedition met with a like fate.
Although we have no positive evidence, there are con-
verging hints and side-winds which suggest that some
of the explorers reached the American coast and followed it far enough southwards to excite considerable
alarm in Spain. If they did so, we know that they did
not find the cities of Cathay. In England there is no
record whatsoever of the fortune of the voyage. Perhaps no news ever came. If news did come, it was of
disappointment, for there were no spices. These projectors were intent on profitable trade, and set little
store by interesting discoveries in pure geography.

In his first voyage Cabot had found what we know to
have been a new continent, although he had supposed
it to be an old one. The effective discovery of America,
as a factor in European history, took place when
Cabot's erroneous belief was discredited; and it is not
easy to say precisely when that was. We have now to
examine the circumstances which indicate the change
of view. For the evidence is circumstantial. We have
no sudden and universally accepted reversal of opinion,
nor even a period of obvious controversy. The truth
slipped almost silently into the general consciousness.
The idea that this western continent was not Asia but
something new was evidently being formed some time
before it was boldly formulated. It involved so radical
a change in geographical conceptions that men shrank
from committing themselves. Its earliest manifestations
are to be inferred from their actions, and not from their

[1] Denys Hay, 'The Manuscript of Polydore Vergil's Anglica Historia',
English Hist. Review, April 1939.

recorded writings or maps. Next there was a phase in which some sought a compromise, which should partly preserve the validity of the old ideas, although others realized that no compromise was possible. Not until nearly twenty years had passed did the American continents stand forth in general European thought unmistakably in the form in which we know them.

It appears likely that the English early divined the truth, and the lost record of Cabot's second voyage may be the missing clue to their effective discovery of America.

On his first expedition the explorer had seen no Asiatic civilization, in fact he had seen no inhabitants of any sort. But he had then considered himself to be only in the outlying part of Cathay where trade and cities were not to be looked for. On his second attempt he confidently expected to find them, farther south, in the tropical latitudes to which he was bound. If any of his people went down the American coast and came home to tell the tale, they must have returned disillusioned. So much can be said without a doubt. We do not know that they returned, but the subsequent actions of the English square with the supposition that they did, and are less easily reconciled with the alternative, that no news ever came.

In either case the voyage was a financial failure, and the enthusiasm of London died away as quickly as it had arisen. The Bristol men were much more persevering and believed that the West still had possibilities. They had lost with Cabot the Italian inspiration, and their maritime connexion with Portugal again asserted its influence.

In the western outpost of the Azores there was an established Portuguese colony, whose active men were inevitably seamen and thought much of new discoveries. One such Azorean captain, João Fernandez of Terceira, is reported to have made explorations before Columbus, with results now unknown. But the Portuguese of the islands thought of more islands rather than of the road to Asia, and Fernandez, true to type, obtained a patent from the King of Portugal in 1499, giving him the governorship and revenues of any islands he might discover. A few months afterwards, before Fernandez had had much time to act, his grant was superseded by a new one to a man of higher rank, Gaspar Corte Real, a nobleman of Terceira, who obtained the sole leadership of future Atlantic effort. João Fernandez, thus dispossessed, betook himself to England, and entered into alliance with the merchants of Bristol, in which port he or someone of his name had been trading long before. With him were two other Azoreans, Francisco Fernandez and João Gonsalvez.

The result of the alliance was that early in 1501 Henry VII issued to the three Azoreans and to three Bristol merchants a patent conferring upon them the monopoly of trade with any new lands they might discover, previously unknown to Christians. The coasts that John Cabot had discovered, from Newfoundland southwards, were therefore excluded, since they were not unknown to Christians. Neither was Cabot's patent cancelled, and even if his death was now presumed, his rights were hereditary and descended to his sons. It follows then that the new combination intended to operate north of Cabot's area, and that is a light on the discovery of America. It suggests that the new coast was recognized not to be Asia and that the enterprise was to seek a way round it by the north. It suggests that, but by no means proves it; although in support we may consider that all emphasis had hitherto been upon discovery in warm climates, and that northern lands can have offered little attraction for their own sakes.

The new syndicate made voyages in 1501 and 1502

with results that seemed promising, since Henry VII granted substantial money rewards to the merchants, and pensions to two of the Azoreans. The service thus rewarded was described as exploring in 'the New Found Land'. The phrase is significant. Cabot had claimed reward for finding the empire of the Grand Khan, but in 1502 we have no suggestion of Asia. 'The New Found Land' is henceforward the designation of all the western coasts, not merely of the part now called Newfoundland.

At the end of 1502 the King issued yet another patent naming two of the Azoreans and two Bristol men and giving them much more extensive rights. They were now empowered not only to discover new lands but to 'recover' others previously known. In fact, the only regions from which the patent debars them are those actually in the possession of foreign sovereigns in amity with the King. This proviso is very important. From the outset Henry VII had disregarded the papal assignment of all the unknown world to Spain and Portugal. But he had respected the rights of prior discovery; and the earlier patents, by limiting the grantees to lands unknown to Christians, had forbidden trespass in the regions found by Spain and Portugal. Now, in 1502, Henry no longer bound himself by that limitation, and substituted for it the doctrine of effective occupation. He would respect actual possession by other European powers, but nothing else. The syndicate of 1502 became known as The Company of Adventurers to the New Found Lands. It sent out expeditions for at least four years. But we have no exact information of their destination or purpose. Circumstantial evidence, not conclusive, suggests that they were searching for the North West Passage, which would imply that the New Found Land was recognized not to be Asia, but a barrier on the road to Asia.

By the date of Cabot's first voyage Portugal was committed to the project of reaching the Far East by the Cape of Good Hope; and while Cabot was crossing the Atlantic Vasco da Gama set out on the expedition which took him round the Cape to India. When Cabot came home asserting that he had been to Cathay and back in three months, Portugal was naturally interested. In 1498 King Manuel sent out an expedition to investigate what Cabot had discovered.[1] This expedition reached some part of the American coast and thence returned, and no details of its proceedings have been preserved. From what followed it seems probable that this exploration satisfied the Portuguese that the western land was not Asia; for their next undertaking was to sail northwards towards the Arctic. Vasco da Gama came home from India in 1499. He had been successful, but his voyage had occupied two years. And as soon afterwards as possible Gaspar Corte Real sailed from Lisbon to Greenland. He pressed up its eastern coast until stopped by ice, and then tried its western coast, also without success. What could have been the object of this northern exploration? The answer seems unavoidable, that it was to see whether a polar passage was open to Asia; and that could only have been on the understanding that the New Found Land was not Asia. Gaspar Corte Real tried again in 1501 between Greenland and Labrador, in the gateway now called Davis Strait, which has led so many explorers to the search for the Passage. On this occasion Corte Real and his ship were missing, lost, like John Cabot, in some unknown disaster, although two of his consorts came home. Miguel Corte Real, his brother, sailed in 1502 on the same quest, and he also disappeared. The North Atlantic took heavy toll of its explorers.

So far we have been examining suggestive clues to the

[1] Duarte Pacheco Pereira, *Esmeraldo de Situ Orbis*, ed. G. H. T. Kimble, Hakluyt Soc., 1937, p. 12.

question of the recognition of America, but they have
not amounted to certainty. Certainty, so far as the
English are concerned, is found in 1509. In that year
Sebastian Cabot, son of John, a young man of about
twenty-four, who had been living at Bristol since his
father's death, sailed on an expedition which was quite
positively for the purpose of finding the North West
Passage to Cathay. He passed through Hudson's Strait
and entered Hudson Bay.[1] He believed that he had
sailed completely round the New Found Land and that
the sea route to Asia lay clear before him. But the ice
was formidable, and the peril and hardship caused his
men to insist on return. Here is sufficient proof that the
English saw America in its true light, as a land distinct
from Asia, by 1509, even if they had not done so ten
years earlier.

But in England there were as yet no scientific geographers of the sort that published their results and their
speculations. Even Sebastian Cabot long concealed
what he knew, as a secret to remain in cold storage until
he should find an opportunity to exploit it. To complete this examination of the effective discovery of
America we must consider when the truth became
common property to educated Europe.

Columbus, as we have seen, had claimed in his first
voyage that Cuba was part of the mainland of Asia.
Doubts soon arose, even among the Spaniards, although
their leader continued to assert the identification. His
friend Andres Bernaldez, the priest who wrote a sym-
pathetic account of his voyages, told him in 1496 that
another 1,200 leagues to the westward would not bring
him to Asia;[2] and this was substantially the view of John

---

[1] For an examination of the evidence for this statement, see the
author's *Voyages of the Cabots*, London, 1929, ch. ix.
[2] *The Four Voyages of Columbus*, ed. Cecil Jane, Hakluyt Soc., 1930,
p. 116.

Cabot. In 1503 the editor of the first Spanish version of Marco Polo declared in his introduction that the newly discovered islands to the west were not the islands of Asia, but far from it;[1] and from that date onwards the publication of the voyages of Amerigo Vespucci accustomed men to think of the discoveries as a *mundus novus*.

Maps are of course a species of evidence on this matter to which we naturally turn, and Spanish maps might be especially enlightening. Unfortunately only one relevant Spanish map of this crucial period has been preserved. It was made in 1500 by Juan de la Cosa, an officer who had sailed three times to the western discoveries. La Cosa delineates the western land as a continent stretching from the Arctic circle to the tropic of Capricorn, but his map is so arranged as to avoid stating whether the continent is to be regarded as a new land-mass or a part of Asia. It is evident that the cartographer is either uncertain on the question, or does not desire to make a positive statement. The same ambiguity appears in other large maps of 1502 and 1503, prepared in Portugal. The first clear statement of a separate America occurs in the well-known Inset Map printed by Martin Waldseemüller of Strasbourg in 1507. Here North and South America joined by their connecting isthmus are drawn, with the Atlantic Ocean on one side and a new ocean, not yet named the Pacific, on the other. Waldseemüller, a purely academic geographer, had hit upon the essential truth; and his was the first published work to distinguish America from Asia.

Others were not so advanced. Contemporaries of Waldseemüller continued to draw maps on the old tripartite theory, showing the western continent as

[1] Rodrigo Fernandez de Santaella, ed. N. M. Penzer, London, 1929, pp. 5–9.

identical with Asia. Many sought to reconcile the conflicting views by describing the Americas as a vast outgrowth of Asia, jutting eastwards from it and then southwards, so that they formed a barrier to reaching Marco Polo's Cathay, and yet were physically continuous with it. This conception was almost equivalent to regarding America as a distinct continent, and we may visualize it by imagining a modification of our present maps, whereby Alaska and Siberia should be connected by an isthmus instead of being separated by a strait.

There was a religious hindrance to accepting complete separation. It had been observed that the western aborigines possessed only canoes with paddles, and did not know the use of sails. It seemed unlikely that they had been able to cross an ocean. How, then, had their stock been planted in America? For they were human beings, and must be descendants of Adam. This doubt remained unsolved, and was simply shelved as the evidences of a separate America grew increasingly strong. In 1508 the Portuguese geographer Duarte Pacheco, who had been a member of the western expedition sent out ten years before, wrote that the world held not three continents but four, and that the fourth was the western land extending through a hundred degrees of latitude;[1] while of the natives he remarked, 'and now it only remains to know if they are descended from Adam'. A decade later, in 1519, the Englishman John Rastell, while having no doubt of the separation, still alluded to the awkward problem which sprang from it: 'But how the people first began in that country, and whence they came, for clerks it is a question.'[2] That is the latest reference discovered to the theological importance of the native American; for by 1519 the clerks were about to join issue over matters of greater moment.

[1] *Esmeraldo, ut supra*, 12–15.
[2] John Rastell, *A New Interlude*, &c., London, c. 1519.

We may regard the first decade of the sixteenth century as the period of indecision and dispute on the nature of the western continent. Those who had seen it, Columbus excepted, believed it to be something hitherto unheard of; while the scholars of Italy and Germany, Waldseemüller excepted, clung to the Ptolemaic conception of the tripartite world and grafted the newly found coast-lines upon the eastern Asia described, but not mapped, by Marco Polo. Observation of the facts ultimately produced agreement. As every year brought more knowledge both of America and of Asia, it became increasingly evident that they could not be the same. There was no outstanding pronouncement that secured immediate consent, but only a gradual conversion of opinion. Well before 1520 the tripartite theory was dead; America was clearly discovered, by England and by all Europe; and the maritime enterprise of western Christendom saw displayed an Old World and a New, whose exploitation was to yield work, wealth, and dominion to the white race for four centuries to come.

II

ENGLISH ENTERPRISE IN THE ATLANTIC

FOR two hundred years after the discovery of America the chief efforts of English expansion were in the Atlantic, and especially in the North Atlantic. Indeed, by the beginning of the eighteenth century that area had developed almost into a British lake. The present lecture will review the leading features of the process by which it did so.

America, when first effectively discovered, was a disappointment to all concerned, for it blighted the hopes of an easy westward contact with the wealth of Asia. It was a barrier, and it seemed to offer few attractions of its own. Its habitable lands were of little interest to Renaissance Europe, which had no surplus population desirous of emigrating. The glory of territorial conquest made some appeal to the knightly adventurers of Spain, as did the glory of spreading Christianity among the heathen, but even these motives had little permanent weight unless reinforced by that of material gain. With the other nations concerned the predominant motive was simply trade, and America at first appeared to offer very little.

To this general unattractiveness of America exceptions began to appear. The Newfoundland fishery was one of the first. Western Europe had hitherto drawn its greatest supply of salt fish from the coast of Iceland, visited every summer by hundreds of small vessels. Fishermen from all parts of England had worked the Iceland coast, but after Cabot's discovery the west countrymen gave it up and resorted to Newfoundland instead. Men from Bristol and Devon so multiplied their energies in Newfoundland that they not only supplied England with fish but developed an export trade in it. But the fishery long remained the only fruit of English discovery, and the rest of North America lay derelict of our enterprise for nearly a century.

Farther south the Caribbean formed a unit of interest, an annexe of the Atlantic fringed by islands and by the shores of the continent from Florida round to the mouth of the Orinoco. In the Greater Antilles the Spaniards were at first encouraged by finding gold. They soon exhausted the supply, but not before they had destroyed the native population in the slavery of mining it. In general the Antilles yielded the first generation little but hardship, and many a despairing adventurer cursed Columbus for finding them. The chief Spanish hope in the Caribbean was to find a way out of it, by means of some channel leading westwards to Asia. Columbus vainly searched the coast-line of Central America, and at a later date expeditions from Cuba visited the Gulf of Mexico. They found no sign of a strait, but they did hear of the rich and semi-civilized empire of the Aztecs in the interior.

This news, obtained a quarter of a century after the primary discovery of 1492, opened a new chapter in American enterprise. The continent became for the first time attractive to the Spaniards. Cortés conquered Mexico and sent home its treasure. Then his followers settled down to work its silver-mines, and it became the Viceroyalty of New Spain, the first continental dominion of the Spanish Empire. The process spread to South America. Pizarro founded the second wealthy Viceroyalty of Peru, and the Isthmus of Panama became important as the link between two oceans, giving land-portage in default of a strait on the treasure-route from Peru to Spain. In the half-century after Cortés began his conquest, Mexico and Central America and the western half of South America became a Spanish empire.

The eastern angle of South America was more gradually developed by the Portuguese. Cabral, sailing southwards after Vasco da Gama, discovered it in 1500. Its red dye-woods appeared to be its best commodity, and so it was named the Land of Brazil. The word brazil, an old term for dye-stuffs, had long hovered over mythical Atlantic islands, and now at last it found a permanent habitation as a proper name. Portugal showed no great enthusiasm for Brazil for some thirty years, but did at length decide to colonize it as a means of repelling the English and the French from the dye-wood trade. In fact there was gold waiting to be mined within reach of the coast, but the Portuguese did not discover it until the seventeenth century.

In sum, therefore, the Americas assumed a new character as regions valuable for their own sakes, very slowly in the north, where the fishery remained the only exception to complete neglect; very rapidly and sensationally in the centre and in all the parts accessible through the Caribbean; and with moderate development in Portuguese Brazil, which long remained only a trading coast and by no means a dominion comparable with New Spain or Peru.

The eastern side of the Atlantic had a different history. In a sense the Portuguese problem was simpler than the Spanish, for the ambition of the Portuguese was more limited. They talked of the conquest and conversion of Africa, but in practice were content with its trade. Thus the Portuguese occupation of tropical Africa consisted of a few forts and trading factories scattered at wide intervals along the coast. There was very little conversion of the negroes, and certainly Christianity was not the rule with them, as it became with the Indians under Spanish authority. Conversion was in practice an aspect of conquest. It was pursued strenuously by Spain in the West, but not by Portugal in Africa, where there were consequently no Portuguese dominions.

West Africa was easily accessible from Europe, and the Portuguese monopoly was soon challenged. The Spaniards were the first trespassers, but the two countries came to terms by the Treaty of Alcaçovas in 1479. This treaty was of permanent importance, for by it Castile recognized the monopoly of Portugal on the African coast, and also her possession of all the island groups of the eastern Atlantic except the Canaries. So far as the islands are concerned, the treaty has never been infringed. Not for an hour in four and a half centuries have the Canaries been out of Spanish ownership, or the Azores, Madeira, and the Cape Verdes out of Portuguese, and this constitutes a record in the durability of colonial agreements.

A second treaty of still greater historical importance was that of Tordesillas in 1494, whereby Spain and Portugal regulated the problem arising from the discovery by Columbus of new land in the West. For some forty years Portugal had been in possession of papal bulls conferring upon her the monopoly of the conquest and navigation of Africa as far as the Indies. The navigation was in the undefined Atlantic, and the Portuguese saw no reason why it should not comprise the whole width of that ocean, more especially as Columbus claimed that its farther shore was veritably that of the Indies. Portugal therefore protested. Spain appealed to the Spanish pope, Alexander VI, and obtained the bulls of 1493, which allotted to Castile the same rights in the West as Portugal already enjoyed in the East. It was necessary to define these spheres, and the second of the bulls did so by fixing as the dividing line the meridian passing 100 leagues west of the Azores and the Cape Verde Islands. Portugal was still dissatisfied, and the result was the further negotiation at Tordesillas, whereby the papal line was moved to 370 leagues west of the Azores. This location gave the Portuguese their title to Brazil, their only foothold in America. Spain and Portugal continued to observe the principle of the line of demarcation, and in later times jointly strove to enforce it as a monopoly against the English, French, and Dutch, who had not been parties to the original bargain. Thus were formed the two rival groups of maritime powers whose hostilities decided the fate of colonies in the next two hundred years.

The foregoing considerations provide the background upon which the activities of England took shape.

During the greater part of the sixteenth century the governing condition of English enterprise in the Atlantic was the long-standing alliance between the English and Spanish crowns. Concluded by Henry VII and Ferdinand and Isabella at the Treaty of Medina del Campo in 1489, this alliance continued, with two or three short lapses into hostility not amounting to war, until 1569, when it was substantially ended by English sympathy with the Revolt of the Netherlands and Spanish patronage of the pretensions of Mary Stuart to Elizabeth's throne. The original treaty of 1489 promised mutual freedom of trade in all the dominions of the contracting parties, which included the Canary Islands, Spanish property for the past ten years. Englishmen were thus legally free to trade with their own shipping in the Canaries, and regularly did so; and it was stated by Thomas Nicholas, an English factor at Teneriffe, that many English adventurers took part with the Spaniards in the conquest of the aborigines, and settled down as landowners in the islands.[1] Further than this, Spain was tolerant, to a limited extent, of English enterprise in her American colonies. There was at Seville a

[1] E. G. R. Taylor, Introduction to Roger Barlow's *A Briefe Summe of Geographie*, Hakluyt Society, 1932, p. xxi.

community of English merchants. These men were
permitted to ship their goods under the Spanish flag
to the Caribbean, and even to reside in the colonies.
Their ships were occasionally chartered for the colonial
trade, but they were never allowed to sail under their
own flag direct from England to Spanish America. We
have record of two English merchants from Seville
accompanying a Spanish exploring expedition in 1526,
and of another carrying on trade in Hispaniola at the
same date; while somewhat later there were many residing in Mexico and passing freely to and from that
colony in the Spanish fleets. These Seville Englishmen
permeated the Spanish Empire and were an important
agency in making its secrets known to England. In the
reigns of Henry VII and Henry VIII they prospered
on the *entente cordiale* between the two nations. Later,
when England became officially Protestant, their position grew difficult. They had to behave as strict Catholics in Spain, and were contemned accordingly when
they came home. Richard Hakluyt wrote of them that
they were necessarily hypocrites in one country or the
other, and denounced the trader who 'in England
cometh here devoutly to the Communion, and sendeth
his son into Spain to hear Mass'.[1]

Religious conformity and sailing under Spanish
colours were the price exacted even in the days of
friendship for English entry into Spanish America.
Spanish claims included North America so far as to
comprise the coast-line of the later United States, but
Spain never sought to enforce a monopoly of Newfoundland. The reasons for this can only be inferred,
for she never made a statement of policy on the point.
By the principle of the bulls and the Treaty of Torde-

[1] Richard Hakluyt, 'Discourse of Western Planting', in *The Original
Writings and Correspondence of the two Richard Hakluyts*, ed. E. G. R. Taylor,
Hakluyt Society, 1935, p. 221.

sillas the line of demarcation ran from pole to pole, and
it is so represénted in several Spanish maps. There was
a difficulty in establishing the longitude of Newfoundland, and in the early years Portugal claimed it as being
on her side of the line, as it very nearly is. She soon
dropped the claim, and Spain never took it up. A
possible reason is that neither country wished to establish a colony so far north, while it was impracticable
without great expense to assert a monopoly of the fishing
waters. Thus the fishery settled down as a common
industry for Spaniards and Portuguese, Englishmen
and Frenchmen, and before long the two latter nations
divided much the greatest share. By the middle of the
century we find that Spain had tacitly dropped the
claim to monopoly north of her own latitudes, in spite
of the line upon the maps, for in 1555 Philip II as king-
consort of England consented to the issue of the letters-
patent which granted to the Muscovy Company full
rights of discovery and trade in all regions of the north,
north-east, and north-west.

As we have seen, a condition of the Anglo-Spanish
amity was that no direct trade was permitted between
England and Spanish America; and until the very last
years of the alliance English governments discouraged
English ships from sailing to the Caribbean. There was
but one exception in 1527, when Henry VIII was mo-
mentarily on bad terms with Charles V. In that year
the English king sent two ships to seek the North West
Passage. One of them, having failed in the quest, sailed
south to the Caribbean. She visited Porto Rico and
Hispaniola, and her people declared that their King
had sent them to investigate the possibilities of trade.
The Spaniards warned them off, and they departed,
threatening to come again in greater force. They never
did so, and that was the end of the matter. Apart
from this incident, the English Crown felt bound by its

European interests to avoid giving serious offence to Spain.

There was no similar inhibition relating to Portugal. Frenchmen were early trespassers in Brazil, and from 1530, if not earlier, Englishmen from Plymouth and Southampton followed their example. William Hawkins of Plymouth combined the Brazil voyage with calls at the Guinea coast for ivory; and by 1542 the Southampton men had a fortified station of their own in Brazil. After a dozen years we lose sight of this trade, but that is no proof that it ceased; certainly there was a generation later a vigorous English community trading in Brazil, and voyages were commonly made thither. Henry VIII encouraged William Hawkins in his trespasses, and allowed him to exhibit his booty at Court. England had as yet no desire for colonization, and the object of these expeditions was solely to obtain rare commodities. By the middle of the century, when international order had decayed, that object was more easily attained by plain piracy in home waters, and from 1546 onwards the Portuguese made continuous complaint of the plundering of their ships conveying tropical produce from Lisbon up Channel to Antwerp.

The Tudor period is for many purposes sharply divided at the death of Henry VIII, and this division holds good in the pursuit of oceanic expansion. Up to that point enterprise had sprung chiefly from Bristol and the western ports, and even after it the majority of those Spaniolized Englishmen who went to mass in Seville were merchants of Bristol. But from 1547 onwards the general emphasis shifts rapidly to London, not only because London men were becoming adventurous, but also because west-countrymen found it advisable to work from London in order to be in closer touch with government and capitalists. The circumstances of the country were changing. The enclosures, the interruption of old trades by European wars, the rise of prices caused by the flow of American silver into Europe, religious unsettlement, and the break-down of old social relationships, were combining to cause a period of poverty and discontent; and it seemed that the discovery of new trades was vitally necessary to the national survival. The successors of Henry VIII, and notably the Duke of Northumberland, tackled the problem with vigour and some success; and there is a surprising contrast between Northumberland the greedy and unprincipled domestic statesman, who justly perished for his misdeeds, and Northumberland the man of vision and foresight, responding to the appeal of the wide world beyond Europe, the patron of geographers and seamen, the originator of that outburst of enterprise that we regard as characteristically Elizabethan.

Northumberland and his associates employed two expert advisers of the first rank: Sebastian Cabot, by that time an old man of varied experience, supreme in his knowledge of tropical commodities and the navigation and seamanship of long voyages; and John Dee, a rising scholar, whose reading of academic and scientific geography was exhaustive. With their counsel a project of economic salvation was formed, and the first English joint-stock company, chartered by the Crown and financed by the merchants of London, dispatched the Willoughby and Chancellor expedition of 1553 to seek markets for English cloth along the north coast of Asia. A small but solid success was attained by the discovery of the White Sea and entry into unknown Russia. The company became the Muscovy Company and prospered, and in its small sphere provided employment for the starving craftsmen of England.

Meanwhile the same statesmen and the same merchants, with Sebastian Cabot in collaboration, were

opening new trades in the Atlantic. In 1551 they sent
Thomas Wyndham to sell English goods in western
Morocco, and this business also took root and flourished.
Next they secured a Portuguese pilot who knew the
Gold Coast and sent him to guide Wyndham thither
in 1553. William Hawkins, under Henry VIII, had
been only to the modern Liberia, which yielded ivory
but not gold, and no English ship had yet ventured
round Cape Palmas to the long auriferous shore
where the negroes were eager to welcome English goods
and pay for them with glittering gold dust. The new
voyage was also a success, although fever killed Wyndham and most of his men; and the Guinea trade became
the most brilliantly lucrative of the new enterprises.
Northumberland also had views of attacking Spanish
America, but his time was too short. Yet we must
confess that in his four troubled years he had achieved
much.

Under Philip and Mary all these enterprises continued. Philip, as we have seen, gave his countenance
to the northern expansion. He tried hard to stop his
English subjects from going to tropical Africa, but was
unsuccessful, and the reason undoubtedly was that all
English officials, from the Lords of the Council downwards, sympathized with the trespassers. And so we
find that in spite of royal prohibitions the Gold Coast
trade continued and ships of the Royal Navy were
chartered, with the Lord Admiral's connivance, by the
merchants concerned.

When Elizabeth succeeded to the throne she immediately legalized the African trade. The Portuguese
sent three successive embassies to protest, but under
Burghley's advice the Queen asserted the doctrine of
effective occupation. She was informed, she said, that
in most parts of the coast the negroes were not under
Portuguese rule, and she would not prohibit her subjects

from trading with independent peoples by whom they were welcomed. When the ambassador sought to argue that his sovereign was the effective ruler of the whole coast, the Queen retorted that if such were the truth he could settle the matter himself by forbidding his black subjects to trade with the English. Burghley's attitude to the dispute is not in doubt. He was by no means the pacifist that he has sometimes been depicted. He personally conducted the negotiations and formulated the hard doctrine described. He certainly disapproved of piracy and privateering, but he was in favour of pushing legitimate trade. The interpretation of 'legitimate' was, of course, the crucial point. He admitted the right of the Portuguese to exclude Englishmen from their possessions, but he said that the only admissible possessions were those effectively occupied. To Burghley the papal bulls of partition had no validity, as he plainly told a Spanish ambassador as well as the Portuguese. And this was not solely a Protestant defiance, for Francis I had said the same to Charles V.

Before turning to other matters, we may follow the Guinea dispute some way farther. In the 1560's the English were uncompromising, and by 1569 a state of actual, although undeclared, war existed with Portugal. Meanwhile the futility of protest had compelled the Portuguese to extend their scanty fortifications to other parts of the coast, and also to patrol it with armed squadrons. The gold supply was always limited, and interloping was on the increase, with a consequent fall in profits, while England was drifting into serious difficulties with Spain. In the seventies, therefore, the English government grew more accommodating. The Queen, without admitting a change of principle, began to prohibit expeditions to Guinea, and in 1576 she signed a treaty with Portugal whereby it was merely implied that the tropical intrusions were to cease, but clearly stated that Englishmen were free to trade with Madeira and the Azores, as they had long been with the Canaries.[1] This half-settlement did not long endure. Four years afterwards Philip II conquered Portugal, and when in 1585 Spain went to war with England, Portugal was simultaneously involved. English undertakings in Guinea recommenced, if indeed they had ever ceased, and the trade went on until it issued in the foundation of permanent English factories in the seventeenth century. In sum, the English of the Tudor period established a firm hold upon the commerce of the eastern Atlantic.

One African activity, and ultimately the most important, has hitherto not been mentioned, because it involved America also; and that is the trade in slaves. From the first settlement of the Antilles the Spanish government was moved to humane indignation by the sufferings inflicted on the aborigines by the gold-hunting pioneers. This early Spanish humanitarianism must be distinguished from the broader European movement of the eighteenth century. It was concerned with cruelty to the soul rather than to the body. It did not object to slavery but to Indian slavery. For the Indian deprived of his liberty died in sullen despair, cursing the god of the white man, and, so dying, was indubitably damned. The African, on the other hand, made the best of his lot, throve in servitude, and gratefully accepted salvation. To carry off negroes from heathen Africa was to confer upon them an inestimable benefit, for which a temporary mundane hardship was a small price to pay. This happy disposition of the negro was well known before the discovery of America, and so on all grounds it seemed reasonable to fill the Caribbean

[1] J. W. Blake, *European Beginnings in West Africa, 1454–1578*, London, 1937, ch. viii.

mines and plantations with negro slaves and spare the
Indians for conversion by kinder means. The negroes
had to be obtained from Guinea, and the method was
by the sale of contracts for fixed numbers at fixed prices
to various mercantile firms, sometimes Spanish, but
more often Portuguese, Italian, or Flemish. The con-
tractors had, of course, to buy their slaves directly or
indirectly from the Crown of Portugal.

The entry of John Hawkins into the slaving business
marks the entry of England into direct Caribbean enterprise. Although a Plymouth man, he moved to London
and there conducted his operations in close contact
with the minister, Burghley, who maintained a general
supervision of the undertaking, with the government
officials and City merchants who financed it, and with
the Spanish ambassador whose goodwill he persistently
sought. For Hawkins had no desire to enter the Caribbean as an interloper in defiance of Spain, although
that was what he speedily became. He wished to be
a recognized contractor, and the price he offered was
the service of his fighting ships against the enemies of
King Philip. Those enemies were the Turks in the
Mediterranean and the French corsairs who had been
raiding the Caribbean and plundering its treasures for
thirty years past. The Spanish colonists were crying
out for defence, which their government seemed unable
to supply, and there were Spanish officials who regarded
Hawkins as a friend. But Philip would not consent.
Hawkins was not prepared, like the Catholic Englishmen in Spain, to work from Seville under the Spanish
flag and regulations. He required a free hand; and the
King could not agree to allow a direct trade from
England by men who would not conform to his Church
and his highly organized system of imperial control.

Hawkins did not spend long years as a suitor at the
court of Spain. He acted at once in anticipation of the

permission which he was confident of obtaining. Between 1562 and 1568 he organized four expeditions by fleets of increasing size. He obtained his slaves in Africa in defiance of the Portuguese government and in accordance with Elizabeth's clearly stated policy. He sold them in America, without Philip's permission, it is true, but in friendly collusion with the King's officers, with the utmost expressed deference to the King's authority, and with repeated protestations of his desire to do the King a service. Elizabeth gave Hawkins her approval, officially recognized him as her officer, lent him her ships, and allowed him to sail under her royal standard. She thought the project feasible, and she was not then at all desirous of hostilities with Spain. The end was disaster. In 1568 Hawkins was attacked and overwhelmed in the Mexican harbour of San Juan de Ulua, by a superior force under a flag of truce. It was an immensely significant event which, with others in Europe at the same juncture, marked the end of the Anglo-Spanish alliance. The Queen's ships under the royal standard had been destroyed by the King's officers led by his highest servant, the Viceroy of New Spain. But the English were in the Caribbean, and in one capacity or another they have been there ever since.

The next stage was Drake's, the phase of privateering, reprisal, and all the ingenuities of irregular warfare. A crowd of English captains, denied the regular trade which Hawkins had sought, took revenge by turning to the methods of the French, whom the long Hapsburg-Valois wars had already let loose in the tropic seas. These men were not legally criminals, for reprisals at sea were a perfectly recognized method of securing redress for injuries; and the black treachery of San Juan de Ulua was injury enough, in life as well as goods. This justifies Drake, who had been at San Juan; and Hawkins, who sent out Drake to retaliate; and Andrew

Barker, whose goods had been seized by the Inquisition because their absent owner was a heretic. The privateers kept the Caribbean in a ferment during the eight years after San Juan de Ulua, and then with Drake's voyage of circumnavigation the interest shifted elsewhere. In 1585 he was back in the scene of his first exploits, carrying out the great raid of the Caribbean coasts that marked the opening campaign of the Spanish War.

Meanwhile the western Atlantic in temperate latitudes was at length attracting English enterprise. In 1583 Sir Humphrey Gilbert, after formally annexing Newfoundland in the Queen's name, sought to plant a colony in Nova Scotia. The loss of his colonists by shipwreck foiled the attempt, and his own death in the foundering of the *Squirrel* prevented its renewal. Sir Walter Ralegh followed with expeditions designed to colonize Virginia. The first colony failed and deserted the undertaking. The second, in 1587, promised better, but was ruined by the Spanish War. Naval campaigns absorbed all English shipping for two successive years, and when Virginia was at length revisited the handful of colonists had vanished in some catastrophe which has ever since remained mysterious. The coast-line between the fishery and the Caribbean, alone of the possible spheres of North Atlantic enterprise, remained unfruitful to the end of the Tudor period.

In the work of establishing an English interest in the Atlantic the Spanish War was an interruption of nearly twenty years. It produced some great official expeditions and a vast amount of irregular privateering, but no captured colonies or trading-posts. The real object of the Queen and her ministers was to defend England from revolution and invasion, and their most aggressive use of sea-power was directed to applying damaging pressure to Spain in the hope of securing peace; they did not aspire to the conquest of the Spanish Empire. The enduring results of the war were threefold: thinking men in England became familiar with the possibilities of Atlantic enterprise; Spaniards became at heart disillusioned of the possibility of maintaining their monopoly against vigorous intruders; and Hawkins and Drake created an ocean-going Navy, a new type of armament capable of striking hard blows thousands of miles from home. Their creation was not fully exploited in their own time, nor for fifty years afterwards; but it was not forgotten, and in the second half of the seventeenth century it became an instrument of rapid empire-building.

Under the early Stuart kings there was indeed a remarkable advance, but it was little due to state action. James I and Charles I followed rather than led, and hindered more than they helped. The movement which founded the mercantile Empire was a spontaneous outburst of national energy, a swarming-off of the people such as had never occurred before and has since occurred only once, in the early and middle nineteenth century. The merchants provided capital, and the gentry leaders, but this was nothing new. The unprecedented feature lay in the solid waves of man-power that swept across the Atlantic and in a generation founded a dozen colonies so securely that in every one of them the parent stock preponderates to this day, and its language, politics, laws, and religion have imposed themselves on all subsequent immigrants. Craftsmen and shopkeepers, clergymen and seamen were seized with the desire to roam; but above all it was the husbandmen, the tillers of the soil, who were fired with a new ambition, to forsake all and endure all, to push to the West, to break in virgin soil, to become proprietors and free men, instead of drudges working for a wage, as they must ever remain upon the tightly held fields

of England. We distinguish the Puritan colonies and
the Anglican colonies, the colonies under chartered
companies and those under a Lord Proprietor, but
in truth these distinctions concerned only the leaders.
To the common man it mattered little whether he
went to Massachusetts or Barbados, and he knew little
in advance of the varying conditions between which he
might choose. His governing motive was the hunger
for land, anywhere, in any climate, under any religion.
With that purpose he emigrated, in his hundreds up
to 1625, in his thousands and tens of thousands until
about 1640, when conditions changed and the movement came to a pause. But by that time a new English
stock had been founded, a colonial population, much
more prolific than the old nation, and able to expand
thenceforward by its own fecundity. Theorists of Vic-
torian England talked of 'self-supporting colonization'
as something that they could set going by elaborate
design. The men of early Stuart England practised it
by the light of nature.

Between the Spanish War and the Civil War the
Atlantic colonies were founded. The most important
of them, and the most desirable in the estimation of
statesmen, were those of the plantation type in which
the people farmed, not directly for their own subsistence,
but to produce commodities for sale in Europe; for the
handling of these commodities would enrich the mother
country. The plantation colonies formed a system
which disregards the divisions of modern regional geography. They ranged from Maryland and Virginia on
the northern coast-line and Bermuda in the ocean north
of the Caribbean, southwards through St. Kitts, Nevis,
Antigua, and Montserrat of the Leeward group in the
Antilles to Barbados set rather apart from the others
at the end of the line. This is to mention only the permanent foundations, but there were many others that

failed to take root. The process in fact began with a
settlement in Guiana in 1604, from which date right
through the emigrating period there were persistent
efforts to plant on the Guiana rivers and in the delta of the
Amazon. In the Caribbean there were attempts which
failed at St. Lucia, Grenada, Trinidad, Tobago, Tortuga,
and Santa Catalina, which a Puritan company renamed
Providence and occupied for many years. The failures
were not all loss, for many of the people concerned
moved on to reinforce the successful colonies. In fact
it was a general rule in the Caribbean that once a man
had quitted the ship that brought him from England he
did not go home; he was a colonist for life, and the
father of colonists. He might be an unsuccessful man
who never found the visionary freehold that had
tempted him from his English field; but in the Caribbean he remained, wandering from island to island and
from disappointment to hope.

Of the more settled population in the pioneer years
many became small planters in all the colonies from
Maryland to Barbados, and there were many more of
them in the islands than in the mainland colonies, large
as these latter appear upon the map. The first generation was that of the small planter working with a few
indentured servants, in effect apprentices, on a plot that
seldom exceeded fifty acres. The indentured servant
was the typical poor emigrant, who worked without
wages for a term of years in return for his keep and his
passage out. When he had completed his term he might
secure a plot of his own if there was any suitable
land still vacant. The attractiveness of this prospect
to the landless Englishman undermined the whole
system within twenty years; for by 1640 all the good
land within reach of shipping was everywhere taken up,
and indentured servants no longer volunteered. Access
to shipping was essential to a planter, and these early

settlements have been well described as the tide-water colonies.

The fortunes of the small planter were bound up with two conditions, the supply of cheap indentured labour and the marketing of tobacco. Although there were early experiments with cotton and dye-stuffs, tobacco was everywhere the chief pioneer crop. It could be grown on small plots, it needed no capital expenditure on equipment, and the method of its culture was easily learnt. At first the profits were high. Emigration responded to the call, and very quickly the prospect changed. By 1636 the European markets were flooded with tobacco, and the prices barely yielded a living to the planters. They, it must be remembered, were so intent upon tobacco that they were not growing their own food-stuffs. They relied upon importation of corn and fish, butter and cheese, and also of their shoes and clothes and the strong liquors which they held essential to a good life. The glut of tobacco reduced them to hunger and debt. The planter mortgaged his holding to the merchant-shipowner, who alone could supply his wants, and the period of absentee ownership of plantations set in. By the mid-century it was a common saying that 'the planters are the merchants' slaves'.

In Maryland, under the wise rule of Lord Baltimore, its founder, this result was not pronounced, for the planters from the outset provided their own subsistence, with the tobacco-export as a luxury. In Virginia it was not utterly disastrous, although a good many estates were consolidated and the small planters forced down into the class of employees. In the islands there was a social revolution. The merchant-capitalists turned to a more profitable crop, and introduced sugar-planting. It began in Barbados about 1640, and thence spread to the Leeward group. Sugar killed the small plantation and the free emigration from England. For sugar needed crushing machinery, windmills, costly copper tanks and boilers, wagons and draught-animals, and labour organized in gangs. It was not a small-holder's but a rich man's game. And the rich man, if he was not an absentee, lived as an aristocrat in his great house set in an estate of 500 or 1,000 acres. The small twenty-acre plantations disappeared. Some of their owners remained as wage-earners, but the majority drifted off, to join the buccaneers, to serve in the West Indian wars which Cromwell recommenced, to cut logwood on the prohibited Spanish coast in the Bay of Honduras, to prospect for islands not yet colonized and dispute possession with their Carib inhabitants. In the twenty years after 1640 the Caribbean was in a state of flux, and the swarms of masterless men accumulated, to be the pioneers of new colonies when the ferment subsided.

In the original islands the free white population was heavily reduced. Indentured servants still came out, but in lower numbers and of a different type. Willing emigrants no longer came forward. The servants were henceforward servile, with little hope of eventual prosperity, reprieved criminals, prisoners of war from Drogheda and Worcester, prostitutes swept up in periodical cleansings of the London streets, unlucky children kidnapped by crimps. But these were not the main supply of labour. More and more the planters turned to the negro slave. The merchants who supplied the refining machinery were not all English. Many were Dutch belonging to the great business firms of Amsterdam. Dutchmen were by this time established on the Gold Coast, and it was they who began the intensive pumping of black labour into the English plantations.

The mass-emigration which founded the Caribbean colonies was much less efficiently regulated than that which produced the settlements on the American continent. The method of the Stuart kings was to grant charters to companies or lords-proprietors and allow them to take what measures they thought fit. The result depended greatly on the character of the persons who obtained these comprehensive powers of government. On the whole the continental colonies were fortunate in this respect, but the colonies of the Lesser Antilles were markedly unfortunate. They were granted by Charles I to James Hay, Earl of Carlisle, one of the Scottish courtiers who had entered England in the train of James I. Carlisle was a greedy spendthrift, who gathered huge emoluments in England and yielded no service to the country in return. He regarded his Caribbean proprietorship in the same light, plundering his colonists by every conceivable means and taking no pains to provide justice or a good administration. Neither he nor his successor so long as the patent endured ever crossed the Atlantic to study the conditions in person. The sins of the proprietorship were a large cause of the social unsettlement that was evident even before the economic revolution that arose from the introduction of sugar-planting. The French were at the same time planting Caribbean colonies, and they also were not too well governed: the France of Richelieu was much less orderly and capable of managing distant possessions than that of Louis XIV. The joint result was that many of the failures and displaced planters of both nations withdrew altogether from their allegiance and adopted a new way of life.

A Frenchman, the Abbé Du Tertre,[1] has given us a picture of the outcast type, the emigrants who had failed to take root. They resorted to those parts of the great Spanish islands which Spain had left waste. There

---

[1] Quoted in A. P. Newton, *The European Nations in the West Indies, 1493–1688*, London 1933, p. 169.

they lived in the unsettled regions in bands resembling irregular armies, migrating from place to place as occasion beckoned. These men subsisted by hunting, and never tasted bread or sheltered under a roof. They were clad like sailors in woollen shirts and canvas drawers. They made shoes of raw hide from the wild cattle that they killed, and for camp equipment each man girt a sack about his waist to serve as a sleeping-bag and a defence against nocturnal insects. These hard-living men were already numerous in the 1630's and were continually recruited. To join the 'cow-killers' was the refuge of the colonist from proprietary tyranny or of the sailor who was tired of his ship. The Spaniards on whose neglected lands they trespassed persecuted them, and in retaliation they took to the sea in growing numbers and cruised against Spanish ships. By 1650 they were the sea-going buccaneers, and they remained a terror to the West Indies for the next generation. But times changed, and the buccaneers with them. Their irregular war with Spain degenerated into general piracy, and the government of Charles II used its naval force in the West Indies to put them down. In the 1680's the buccaneers were no longer a Caribbean power. Some of their leaders retired into respectability, like Henry Morgan, who became a knight and deputy-governor of Jamaica. Others led their men to other scenes, and buccaneering thinned out over the Pacific and the Indian Ocean, and ultimately disappeared.

In the middle of the seventeenth century English governments resumed the initiative in Atlantic enterprise which the early Stuarts had dropped. The Commonwealth passed its two Navigation Acts to exclude the Dutch from the colonial trade. Cromwell made a treaty with Portugal in 1654, whereby the English trade with Brazil secured full recognition. At the same time he picked a quarrel with Spain, meditated the conquest of the whole Caribbean empire, and achieved that of Jamaica. Cromwell tried to colonize Jamaica with the soldiers of his expeditionary force, but they nearly all died of fever and privation, in fact of tropical ignorance. Then he bethought him of the surplus colonists elsewhere, and Jamaica was successfully planted by large numbers of seasoned West Indians from Nevis and Barbados. Charles II continued the active policy. He committed to eight proprietors, headed by Clarendon, the task of colonizing the Carolinas; and again this was accomplished by employing the overflow of existing colonists. But Charles II's most notable work was to complete the Commonwealth policy of ousting the Dutch and making the English colonial trade an English monopoly. New Navigation Acts did this in theory, but a war was necessary to enforce it in practice. So long as the Dutch controlled the supply of slaves they were indispensable to the growth of the sugar plantations, and so long as they held New Amsterdam on the American coast they had an entre-pôt for illegal dealings of all sorts. In the war of 1664–7 the English captured New Amsterdam and retained it as New York, while the result of much taking and losing of stations on the African coast was that the English were left with a firm foothold there, and the way was clear for the Royal African Company of 1672 to become the recognized vendors of slaves to the plantations.

Free emigration, as has been said, had ceased with the exhaustion of unoccupied land in the pioneer colonies. Late in Charles II's reign, however, a hitherto overlooked region provided a new opportunity of this sort. The estuary of the Delaware River carried navigable water far into the American interior, and William Penn, the Quaker leader, secured a grant from the King in 1681 and founded Pennsylvania, the first colony without a coast-line upon the open ocean. Penn's Quakers were in one sense free emigrants, but in another sense they went under compulsion, for it was persecution rather than ambition that drove them out. Even so, their numbers were small, and the population of Pennsylvania was largely made up with Swiss and German peasants who were seized with the same land-hunger as had impelled the English half a century before. In England the stimulus was exhausted.

So far nothing has been said of New England, of those sturdy English colonies ruled by Puritans, which were to play so large a part in the founding and fashioning of the United States. They have been left out of the account up to this point because they were no helpful factor to the plantation interest and the English scheme of making the mother country the centre of the web of Atlantic enterprise. Far from being a help, they were in contemporary eyes a detriment. Economists regretted their existence, and if the early Stuart kings had been alive to the accepted doctrines of mercantilism they would have done their utmost to prevent New England from coming into being. Massachusetts, the strongest of the group, to whose type the others conformed, was founded by stiff-necked Calvinist gentlemen who could not endure the England of Charles I. The common belief that persecution drove them forth is not altogether true. They were not harried like the poor Quakers of the Restoration. They went, not because England was intolerant, but because they were. They saw no hope of moulding all England in their likeness, and so they withdrew. They would live in a Calvinist state or none. As a ruling minority they ruled New England with a rod of iron. The majority of their followers were not fanatical, but ordinary men who accepted religion and politics as they found them prevailing. The motive of most of the emigrants was not religious freedom but economic, to acquire land and prosper, to live in better conditions than they could at home. Thus New England became a land of farmers. But its coast-line had good harbours and was clothed with pine and oak. The profits of ship-building and ship-owning were comparable with those of sugar-planting in the south. Before many years had passed the Boston merchant rivalled the farmer as the leading New England type, and Boston ships and seamen permeated the Atlantic. They exported their surplus pork and beef and bread to the plantations, but the bulk of their trade was a carrying trade. They handled the fish of Newfoundland, the tobacco of Virginia, the sugar of Barbados, and the negroes of the Guinea coast; and they did so in competition with London, to the detriment of London profits. Boston became a second metropolis of the Atlantic Empire, and Old England viewed it as a rival only less dangerous than the Dutch.

It has been remarked that the period of intensive emigration in the Stuart century was limited; in fact it almost coincided with the reign of Charles I. Afterwards the stream diminished, and the slackening of contacts helped towards that foundation of a distinct Western stock, an American nation in embryo, which undoubtedly took place in the latter half of the seventeenth century. In some of the island colonies, and notably in St. Kitts, Nevis, and Barbados, the numbers became excessive after the first few years, and there was a surplus ready to re-emigrate. In the continental colonies there was apparently unlimited room, but in fact not so, for the value of land depended on its proximity to good anchorage. Thus New England also produced a surplus eager to find new homes. These redundant West Indians and New Englanders were more prominent than new arrivals from Europe in founding the colonies of the later Stuart period. Jamaica and the Carolinas were chiefly colonized by them, although Pennsylvania was an exception. The re-emigrants were not for the most part original colonists, but the sons of colonists, a colonial-born generation which rapidly lost touch with the English habits and interests that had formed the background of their fathers' lives. Environment, not tempered by close contacts with the mother country, worked a great change in them. The Puritan rulers of New England deliberately severed as many ties as possible. Even in the Civil War they showed no great cordiality to the Parliamentary cause, for they regarded their fellow Puritans at home with some disdain, as weaker brethren who had lacked conviction to abandon all things and leave an accursed land. In the later Stuart period there was hardly any new emigration to New England or return of her sons to the land of their origin. The New Englanders had become Americans who preferred to migrate within America.

The plantation colonies had no religious motives for deliberate severance, but they developed none the less a distinctive way of life and thought. Their climate and employments were foreign to home conditions, and so were the incursions of savages and the use of slave labour. Virginia and Maryland were perhaps the least affected, but even there the distinction grew marked. In the West Indies the proximity of hostile Spaniards and Frenchmen induced an adventurous tendency towards illicit trades and buccaneering, which soon became piracy undisguised. The primary emigration had been so hasty and unplanned that there was no reproduction of the English social order or the traditional reverence for the Church. Many early observers were shocked at the irreligion, drunkenness, dishonesty, and general immorality of the new communities; and such things existing unchecked for a full generation made a clean cut from the traditions of the past. Cultural ties with England were lost, and the chief remaining nexus was that the mother country and the colonists were alike engaged in the common interests of a mercantile empire, and that all contributed to the sea-power which defended those interests.

By the close of the Stuart period the English interest in the Atlantic had taken the shape that it was to retain through the eighteenth century. The ocean was a great lake fringed by European settlements carrying on a variety of enterprises all complementary to one another; and the English share of these holdings, and still more of their trade, had grown preponderant. The prevailing winds and currents made most of the movement circular; it was seldom that a ship came home by the track which she had followed on her outward voyage. Northerly winds prevailed on the nearer side of the Atlantic from Portugal down to Guinea, the north-east trades were constant from Guinea to the Caribbean, westerlies were most common in the belt between North America and the British Isles. There were seasonal variations in these general tendencies, and navigators soon recognized them. For a few weeks after the spring equinox the Newfoundland fishermen might look for a fair wind out from England, although by the time their holds were full the westerlies had set in again to blow them home. The autumn was the best time for a quick passage to Guinea, and when the slaver had collected his cargo there he would reach the West Indies after the dangerous hurricane season had passed. Round the circle moved all its specialized commodities, gathering snowball profits for the merchants and vitalizing the industries of the fixed populations. Manufactures from England went everywhere, cheap stuff for the African slave-dealers, luxuries for the Caribbean sugar-planters, solid goods for the prospering Americans. Sugar and tobacco and dye-stuffs came home, not only for England's consumption but for resale to all Europe. By the eighteenth century the English were growing too luxurious to care much for the Newfoundland fish, and most of it went to the Catholic peoples of the Mediterranean, or southward to feed slaves on the plantations. Carolina specialized in rice, but England in the early days did not eat it, and central Europe took the crop. Salt was an indispensable product, for the great fishery could never be glutted with it; and salt was picked up all round the Atlantic circle, in southern Portugal, in the Cape Verde Islands, on the Venezuela coast, at St. Kitts in the Leeward group. All this enterprise, in its thousands of little sailing-ships, seldom over 200 tons in burden, began and ended in a few home-ports. Bristol and Boston were opposite numbers, New York and others were on a lower scale, but London by far transcended them all.

III

THE PROPAGANDISTS OF THE TUDOR PERIOD

IT may seem an inversion of the proper order of events to survey the actions of the Tudor period first, and afterwards to consider the propaganda connected with them. But in truth this propaganda was for the most part inspired by antecedent actions, and it was not markedly successful in securing the immediate adoption of the policies which it sought to promote. Its chief interest is that it records the effect of the new oceanic revelations upon the minds of thinking men, an effect thence transferred to the consciousness of the nation at large. In the Tudor propaganda we see what advanced minds were pondering and planning in the sixteenth century and also what the mind of the community accepted in the seventeenth. This sequence of cause and effect is well exemplified in the first publication we shall have to notice. It was inspired by an unsuccessful venture into the Atlantic, and it produced no very obvious results in further action; but it probably played its undistinguished part in shaping ideas.

In 1516 Sir Thomas More published his *Utopia*, with its fantasy of a strange state in the then unknown parts of South America. This was not propaganda for English enterprise, but it does give a fair indication that More was aware of recent discoveries and was most likely discussing them with his friends. It is therefore no mere coincidence that his brother-in-law John Rastell should come forward next year as the leader of an expedition for discovery and colonization, and that Henry VIII should have given his countenance to the project. What Rastell did may be briefly told. He obtained an open

letter from the King addressed to all Christian princes
and adjuring them of their friendship to assist John Rastell and his associates engaged upon a voyage to distant
countries. Then in the spring of 1517 he equipped
several ships in the Thames and sailed down Channel
intending to go to North America and make discoveries.
Details and circumstances suggest that he purposed to
plant a settlement, and perhaps also to search for a
western passage to Cathay. A late authority asserts that
Sebastian Cabot supervised the preparations, although
he certainly did not accompany the expedition. He
was then employed in Spain, but paid visits to England;
and since the voyage was to be made to regions examined
by himself and his father, and covered by Henry VII's
grant of privileges to the Cabot family, it is natural that
he should have had a hand in it. However that may
have been, the result was complete failure. Rastell, a
landsman, could assert no authority over his mariners,
who were determined not to proceed across the Atlantic.
He persuaded them as far as Cork, where they mutinied,
set him ashore, and sailed for home.[1]

Rastell remained some time in Ireland. About 1519
he was back in London, where he published a play
entitled *A New Interlude and a Merry of the Nature of the
Four Elements*, in effect a scientific discourse seasoned
with some jests and cast into rhymed verse. A single
imperfect copy of the *New Interlude* exists in the Library
of the British Museum. Some lengthy passages on
America are to our present purpose, for they constitute
the earliest literary description of that country in the
English language.

The word 'America' had been coined twelve years
before by Martin Waldseemüller, and by him applied
only to the southern continent described by Amerigo

[1] For discussion of the evidence on this venture, see the author's
Voyages of the Cabots, London, 1929, pp. 244-8.

Vespucci. Rastell seems to use the name America to include the New Found Land across the North Atlantic, and his is possibly the earliest instance of this application. The land, he says, is a great continent discovered by Englishmen in the reign of Henry VII, and its coast has since been found to be continuous for over five thousand miles. The interior is unknown, but the coast is forested, mostly with fir and pine. On the other side of America there is an ocean separating it from Asia. The farther ocean is not wide, and the distance from the Englishmen's New Found Land to the Empire of Cathay cannot be much more than a thousand miles. In this ocean there may be lands at present unknown. Rastell's view ranges wide, and he speaks also of the unknown possibilities of the southern hemisphere, which may or may not contain an inhabited continent, and even a civilized people—an evident echo of *Utopia*. But his immediate purpose is to suggest English enterprise in North America, which he says he would have initiated but for the despicable mariners who had betrayed him:

> Whiche wolde take no paine to saile farther
> Than their owne lyst and pleasure
> Wherfore that vyage and dyvers other
> Suche kaytyffes have distroyed.

American colonization, he says, would be advantageous for the following reasons: the honour of extending the King's dominions; the conversion of the natives, who as yet know neither God nor the Devil, heaven nor hell; exploiting the wealth of the forests for pitch, tar, and soap ashes now obtained from the Baltic countries; and, finally, for securing the fishery, where foreigners are already lading a hundred ships a year.

It was a modest and reasonable programme, with no promise of glittering gold. And indeed, when Rastell wrote, America was not thought to be auriferous. The news of Mexico was on the way, but had not yet arrived; while Peru was far in the future. What effect the little book had is quite unknown. It is safe to say that the King read it, or witnessed a declamation of the *Interlude*; and More's influential circle were of course in sympathy with it. But we may guess that it had little public circulation; for Richard Hakluyt, the great Elizabethan collector of all such material, appears to have been ignorant of its existence. Henry VIII was from this time anxious to promote Atlantic enterprise. In 1521 he tried to induce the English merchants to finance a national undertaking for America and probably Cathay. The men of Bristol were willing, but those of London hung back; and their opposition, coupled with the outbreak of a French war, caused the plan to be dropped.

Magellan's voyage of circumnavigation took the Spaniards across the Pacific to the Spice Islands of the Far East, and in 1522 the surviving ship came home with a valuable cargo. At once a dispute arose between Spain and Portugal as to whether the Spice Islands were or were not in the Portuguese hemisphere as defined by the Treaty of Tordesillas. Charles V was as much disposed to sell his claim as to exploit it with his own shipping, and a suggestion was unofficially thrown out that the King of England might consider buying it. The English ambassador in Spain, Doctor Edward Lee, afterwards Archbishop of York, was ordered to make inquiries about the spice trade, and he consulted Robert Thorne, a Bristol merchant residing in Seville. The result was a remarkable work of propaganda which had its influence long after its authors were dead.

Robert Thorne, it seemed, had independently been meditating a great plan of English expansion.

Magellan's voyage had demonstrated the vast area of the Pacific, which was now known to be very much wider than the paltry thousand miles assigned to it by John Rastell. Thorne was concerned, not only with the Spice Islands found by the Portuguese, but with the great unknown lands which he thought must exist in the tropical belt of an ocean whose complete emptiness was improbable. Those lands, continent and islands, he regarded as an empire appointed to England if she would rise to her destiny. His father, also named Robert Thorne, had been one of the Bristol merchants who had sailed westward in the time of John Cabot, perhaps actually in the pioneer voyage of the *Matthew*, and had discovered, not Cathay, but the barrier of the New Found Land. Robert Thorne of Seville had been a boy at the time, and grew up to a knowledge, much greater than we now possess, of those subsequent probings into the North West which had endured until Sebastian Cabot's voyage of 1509. He was convinced that the best way into the Pacific was through the polar region, and that a ship might sail over the pole itself. Men had once thought the tropics barred by heat, but now they knew better; and so, he declared, it would be found with the arctic cold : 'there is no land unhabitable, nor sea innavigable.' The unknown, he conceived, lay on the other side of the pole, on the meridian opposite to that of England, descending to the equator in mid-Pacific. Thorne was anxious to learn something of this region. In 1526 Sebastian Cabot, then Pilot-Major of Spain, sailed in command of a Spanish expedition for the Straits of Magellan and the South Sea. Thorne invested 1,400 ducats and secured places for two Englishmen, Roger Barlow, a Bristol merchant, and Henry Latimer, a pilot. They were instructed by Thorne to discover all they could of the North Pacific, question its natives, and obtain copies of their charts, all with a view to establishing the Pacific navigation from the equator to the north pole. Sebastian Cabot was undoubtedly acquainted with these Bristol men, and must have known the purpose for which Thorne's friends were introduced into the expedition. Here it may be said that the ships never reached the South Sea. Cabot turned instead into the River Plate and spent four years exploring the plains of the Argentine.

Before this was known Thorne received, in 1527, the inquiry about the spice trade from the English ambassador. He replied with an account of what he had already done and what he planned; and this 'letter to Doctor Lee', as it is called, survived to become public at a later date. There the matter rested until Cabot came home from the River Plate in 1530. A year before him came Barlow, who, of course, had learnt nothing new about the South Sea. But Barlow and Thorne were more than ever convinced that their project was sound. They bought a large ship for the polar voyage, returned to England, and devised a prospectus to be laid before the King. This is the well-known *Declaration of the Indies*, formerly thought to have been written by Robert Thorne in 1527, but now recognized to be the joint work of Thorne and Barlow in or shortly after 1530. The prose style is distinctly superior to that of Thorne's letter to Doctor Lee, and it thus appears likely that the actual writing of the *Declaration* was done by Barlow, although Thorne was acknowledged as the originator of the enterprise.

The *Declaration of the Indies* is a fine piece of writing, brief and clear and richly worded, instinct with a vibrant conviction of England's destiny and a faith that the King will worthily fulfil it. But it was not at that time fated to bear fruit. Before it could be presented Robert Thorne died in London on Whitsunday, 1532. He was a rich man, and his wealth had been the mainspring of the enterprise. Barlow alone was not able to go on with it, for he had his own fortune still to make. In the ensuing years he and his brothers prospered by services to Thomas Cromwell and shares in the confiscation of Church lands, but it was not until 1541 that the great project could be revived. At that date Barlow presented his plan with a different introduction, a manuscript which he entitled 'A Briefe Summe of Geographie'— the bulk of it translated from a Spanish work—but with the substance of the *Declaration of the Indies* incorporated in its latter pages.[1] This time it seemed as though action was to follow. The King and the Council discussed the northern voyage and negotiated with a pilot from Seville, but in the end it was all allowed to drop. We have hints of its revival in 1546, 1550, and 1551, but no action was taken. Yet the project of Robert Thorne can be reasonably believed to have lived all this time in the minds of ruling men, and we shall hear of it again a generation later still. Barlow himself died in 1554.

The reign of Edward VI was the seed-time of important enterprises, and the Duke of Northumberland was their patron. Yet the effective work was done without much antecedent publicity, on the advice of men like Sebastian Cabot and John Dee, whose minds were of the secretive type. The only appeal to the public came from the pen of Richard Eden, who did not belong to the ruling circle, and who sought to stimulate an interest in expansion in general, but was not concerned with particular projects. Eden was a civil servant who translated foreign works and added matter of his own. His first book, *A Treatise of the New India*, came out in June 1553, with a complimentary dedication to North-

---

[1] For this subject and for Barlow's collaboration with Thorne, see *A Briefe Summe of Geographie*, ed. E. G. R. Taylor, Hakluyt Society, 1932, Introd., *passim*.

umberland as a promoter of English discovery, and an emphasis upon the wealth obtained by the Spaniards from the Indies. The choice of a patron was unfortunate, for within a few weeks the Duke's head had fallen on the scaffold and the reign of Mary had begun. Eden, however, was too small a man to share the ruin of the great, and he retained his post and continued his writings. In his next volume, *The Decades of the New World*, translated from Peter Martyr's famous work, he sought to correct his previous error. It was now September 1555, and Philip of Spain was the Queen's consort. Eden therefore printed some very fulsome adulation of Philip and strong condemnation of the brutishness of England in not showing sufficient affection for him. Eden's style and character were not such as to arouse enthusiasm, and he had no plan for empire-building. But the substance of his books was novel to his public, and their accounts of the wealth of the tropics were the first detailed descriptions that had come from the English press. They were widely read, and we may imagine that they caused many to lick their lips and think thoughts that bore fruit in the time of Drake. Eden's later work dealt with the science of navigation.

In the first decade of Elizabeth the enterprise of her subjects made great advances in the tropical zone of the Atlantic. The Gold Coast trade was actively pursued, and John Hawkins pushed his way with cargoes of slaves into the Spanish colonies of the West. But these activities involved diplomatic trouble with Spain and Portugal, and it was therefore desirable to say as little about them as possible. Thus they evoked little public discussion and no propaganda. At the same time the Muscovy Company, founded by the Duke of Northumberland, was enjoying steady success in its trade with Russia through the White Sea; and more than that, was opening a promising business with Persia by the long overland route through Russia. The Company's charter gave it the monopoly of all exploration to the north of English latitudes, which included the North West and North East Passages, and Thorne's suggested route over the pole. But the Muscovy Company was satisfied to develop its existing commerce, and would promote no new discoveries. This was not to the taste of active men, who thought that there was much to be done in the North; and it was from these men, restive at the Company's inertness, that a new outburst of propaganda proceeded.

Anthony Jenkinson was a distinguished servant of the Company, who had opened the land route to Persia and had travelled far into central Asia. His experiences had convinced him that there could be no regular trade through the continent to Cathay, and he came home to advocate a new voyage for the discovery of the North East Passage. The Company was unwilling, and in 1565–6 Jenkinson appealed over the heads of his employers to the Queen. There were here no diplomatic reasons for secrecy, and he made his suit as public as possible. It was thus an agent in shaping general opinion, although his addresses did not at that time come into print. Jenkinson believed that the northernmost part of Siberia was already known to be accessible to shipping, and that thence the coast fell away southeastwards to the temperate latitudes of the Pacific. His reasons were based on his own experiences: in central Asia he had talked with men from Cathay who had so described their country's coast-line; and in the White Sea he had questioned the native fishermen, who declared that they had been eastwards along the Siberian coast and knew that there was no further obstacle. John Dee had the same belief in the possibility of the North East Passage, but he derived it from quite different evidence, namely, his exhaustive reading of classical and medieval authorities. It is interesting to note that Jenkinson had seen the writings of Robert Thorne and Roger Barlow, for some of his phrases are so obviously echoes of theirs as to constitute plagiarism.

Jenkinson was seeking to goad the Muscovy Company into action. His plans were challenged by Sir Humphrey Gilbert, who also desired to override the Company's monopoly, but for a different purpose. Gilbert was a believer in the North West Passage as the best road to Asia, and he contemned Jenkinson's arguments for the North East. The two men had many conferences, and finally a set debate in presence of the Queen and Council, at which each maintained his own view to his own satisfaction; while the Muscovy Company, which did not intend to do anything, looked smugly on and was able to defend its inaction on the ground that the experts differed. Thus no voyage resulted from the discussion. But some booksellers' records show that it did much to educate public opinion by stimulating an unusual demand for maps and globes,[1] of which some types favoured one passage, and some the other; and it is legitimate to imagine a vigorous public controversy of the sort that would now be carried on by correspondence in The Times. Gilbert himself was moved to cast his arguments into a pamphlet, the celebrated Discourse for a Discovery for a new Passage to Cataia, one of the best-known works of propaganda of the century. Although the Discourse was not printed until 1576, it was composed in the course of the disputation with Jenkinson; and since it was circulated in manuscript, it may rank as a publication of 1566.

Before treating briefly of the Discourse it may be well to indicate a possible source of Gilbert's interest in the subject. He was not, like Dee, a scholar of deep reading,

[1] E. G. R. Taylor, Tudor Geography, London, 1930, p. 99.

neither was he, like Jenkinson, an explorer of wide
experience. He was an active man of soldierly tastes,
who desired to render a great public service to his
Queen and country; and, so far as can be discerned,
his devotion to the cause of the North West Passage was
inspired indirectly by Sebastian Cabot. Cabot, who
claimed to have entered the Passage in his voyage of
1509, had passed his last years in England, where he
died in 1557. Eden had been the old man's friend and
disciple in those latter years, and although he published
no account of the Cabot discovery, he referred to it in
one of his books as a thing beyond doubt. Now in 1562
Eden and Gilbert were thrown together by the circumstance that they both served, the one as a civilian and
the other as a soldier, with the little English army which
went over to help the Huguenots in the defence of Le
Havre. It was after that campaign that Gilbert came
forward as a projector of northern discovery, and the
possibility is that he had talked with Richard Eden and
heard his reminiscences of Sebastian Cabot.[1]

Such is a likely explanation of Gilbert's ambition,
and it supplies the place of a now discredited illusion
about the man himself. For it is now fairly evident that
Gilbert was not a scholar or a student, although he
certainly was a well-educated man. He did not, we
must believe, derive his views from that imposing array
of learned authorities cited in his *Discourse*; on the contrary, he sought out the authorities as backing for views
he had already expressed. The *Discourse* resembles a
case worked up by a lawyer, who takes his side and then
proceeds to marshal all the evidence he can obtain.
Even a casual reading suggests that the author's know-

---

[1] Dr. D. B. Quinn, the most recent authority on Gilbert, allows the
possibility, and justly remarks that it should not be regarded as a certainty. See *The Voyages of Sir Humphrey Gilbert*, ed. D. B. Quinn, Hakluyt
Society, 1940, pp. 4–5.

ledge of these authorities—apart from the well-known classics then read by every man of liberal education—was superficial; and the critical examination made by Professor E. G. R. Taylor reveals that some were misapplied to the strengthening of Gilbert's case, for in fact they contradict it.[1] Even so, the weight of scientific authority is not the main burden of the *Discourse*, which relies chiefly upon deductions from a few simple facts of common acceptance. The deductions are strained, and some of the reasoning is illogical. Gilbert, indeed, had a higher inspiration than he admitted. He was possessed by a faith rather than a demonstrable certainty of the Passage, and he was ready to stake his career upon it. The historical importance of his *Discourse* is that it helped to spread that faith among plain men and to move them to action; and the English interest in the North West Passage was immensely strengthened. For sixty years the North West was virtually an English monopoly. It was barren of any calculable profit, but it convinced the English that their seamen were equal to the hardest tests that the world could offer, and yielded some part of that immeasurable confidence that the ocean was their field of fame. The contrast is seen in the men of Spain and Portugal, who in the early days had shown themselves fit for anything. They clung to their profitable tropics, shirked even their own formidable Straits of Magellan, and steadily slipped back in the world's estimation and their own.

The Straits of Magellan became also for a time an English monopoly, and here we do clearly find propaganda first and action afterwards. There is a possibility resting only on the vaguest hint, that Sebastian Cabot began the interest in it. But, as with much else concerning that remarkable figure, clear evidence has perished. He was always a man without allegiance,

[1] *Tudor Geography*, pp. 34-5.

keeping a foot in either camp, and studiously concealing his tracks. All we know is that in 1558 André Thevet, the French geographer, wrote that a respected English pilot had been talking of the Straits and the southern continent beyond.[1] A few years later the project was in the air, and in 1570 the Spanish ambassador reported that the English government was considering an expedition through the Straits into the South Sea. And then, in the early seventies, it emerges as an empire-building plan of the first importance, the subject of state papers and a propaganda of the semi-confidential kind. Public discussion was precluded, because Spanish susceptibilities were involved.

The promoters were a group of Devon notables with Sir Richard Grenville at their head. He was a fighting man and a man of public affairs, and the extent of his scholarly attainments is even more obscure than that of Gilbert's. But he and his friends were possessed of the latest conclusions of geography about the South Pacific. They believed, and the highest authority supported them, that the land south of the Straits was continental, and that it stretched diagonally across the Pacific to the tropical latitudes south-east of Asia. In this Terra Australis Incognita the newest maps of Mercator and Ortelius marked gold-bearing kingdoms and lands profuse in drugs and spices, while many students of the scriptures were convinced that King Solomon's Ophir lay waiting rediscovery in the same southern area. A Spanish expedition from Peru had even claimed to have found and identified Ophir, and the archipelago which it visited is called the Solomon Islands to this day. The report of the voyage had come to England to confirm the map-makers' assertions. Grenville's syndicate included great landowners of Devon, and

---

[1] André Thevet, *Les Singularitez de la France Antarctique*, Paris, 1878, p. 292 (orig. edn. 1558).

the business talent of the Hawkins firm. Young Captain
Francis Drake was also privy to the plan, a junior then
in wealth and standing, but one who was forming
original views on the command and conduct of the
adventure.

The promoters had no need to argue the geographical premisses, for the passage through the Straits to the
South Sea was already proved, and the existence of
Terra Australis was doubted by none. But they did
set forth attractively 'the commodities to grow of it':
the sale of cloth to the unknown Australians and the
relief of unemployment in England, the likelihood of
finding gold, silver, and pearls, the increase of shipping
and a favourable balance of trade, the spread of Christianity, and above all, the augmentation of England's
power. Had they known it, and it is possible that they
did know, it was the goal proposed by Robert
Thorne to Henry VIII when the century was young.
They concluded by asking the Queen for a charter
allotting to them the monopoly of all new lands to be
discovered in the whole southern hemisphere, the
counterpart of the Muscovy Company's monopoly in
the north. The Pope had partitioned the unknown
world by a meridian; the English Queen was to divide
it by the equator—and to divide it among Englishmen.

The Queen agreed, and the charter was drafted; and
then she changed her purpose, or rather, she considered
where her true purpose lay. In 1574 she had hopes of
a permanent European peace, by mediating between
Philip II and his Dutch rebels and getting the dangerous Spanish army withdrawn from the Netherlands.
This road to a southern empire passed close to the
Spanish treasure-ground of Peru, and Grenville was a
man who would be hard to hold in leash. The North
West Passage offered an inoffensive means of reaching
the Pacific, and that project was coming up again. So

she withheld her consent, and Grenville's plan was postponed for the next three years.[1] By 1577 times had changed, and the Queen had less objection to offending Spain. In that year the expedition sailed for Terra Australis, but Francis Drake and not Grenville was in command. The outcome is well known. Drake, with the Queen's connivance, abandoned empire-building and sacked King Philip's wealth. And by so doing he changed the fashion in South Sea voyages for two centuries to come.

The new plans for the North West were not promoted by Sir Humphrey Gilbert, whom the Queen had employed elsewhere, as a soldier in Ireland and the Netherlands. Two men, well known in other spheres, now came forward to lead the project, Michael Lok, a substantial merchant, and Martin Frobisher, a sea-captain of varied experience, which included a good deal of common piracy in home waters. These two were of old acquaintance, which probably dated from the time when Frobisher, as a boy of fifteen, had served on the Gold Coast in a ship equipped by the Lok family. They had a common interest in their enthusiasm for the North West Passage, and they became close allies in 1574, when the time was favourable to north-western plans as an alternative to Grenville's anti-Spanish schemes for the South Pacific. There is evidence of jealousy between Grenville's Devon syndicate and the Lok–Frobisher combination, which drew its support from London; and when the Queen decided against Grenville she felt bound to give her countenance to his rivals. This accounts for the rapid victory of Lok and Frobisher over obstacles which might otherwise have been insuperable.

[1] For references to the evidence and a more extended discussion of this topic see author's edition of *The Observations of Sir Richard Hawkins*, London, 1933, Introduction, pp. xx–xxviii.

One obstacle lay in Frobisher's piratical past, which had made him unfavourably known to the merchants of London and the Judge of the Admiralty Court. But it had also proved him to be a man of leadership and resource, and in spite of it, he was able to gain the favour of several of the Queen's councillors and, surprisingly, of Burghley, who was in general no lover of pirates. Burghley perhaps regarded the northern ice as a suitable reformatory school, for there was not much piracy to be done there. The other obstacle was the Muscovy Company, which had defeated Gilbert. It still sat tight on its monopoly, and refused to explore the North West or to allow anyone else to do so. Michael Lok had for many years been a member of the Company because he had hoped that it would one day undertake the quest on which his heart was set. He had studied the subject exhaustively, accumulating maps and charts and seamen's tales, and 'a ream of notes', as he tells us, from authorities ancient and modern. When Frobisher applied to the Company for licence, Lok sat on the committee which refused it, although he resented the decision. On the refusal he broke with the Company and threw in his lot with Frobisher. Together they seized the favourable moment and appealed to the Queen; and she issued her royal command to the Company that, in spite of its charter, it must give way. The time was yet far distant when, in such circumstances, the Company could have posed as a martyr to tyranny. It had to submit, without sympathy from anyone.

Lok then carried on a propaganda for funds, and by tact and enthusiasm obtained the support of ministers and courtiers and even the distrustful City merchants who had suffered by Frobisher's piracies. Sir Humphrey Gilbert, home from the wars, was a well-wisher although not an active participant; and a friend of his stimulated the general zeal by publishing the *Discourse* with its arguments brought up to date. Lok, who had not known Gilbert or his book until 1575, welcomed his support, although he modestly pointed out that the *Discourse* contained nothing that he himself had not known for many years.[1]

The outcome was that Frobisher made his first voyage in 1576, and returned to announce, on somewhat flimsy grounds, that he had discovered the North West Passage. He had found also a piece of black mineral which was declared to be gold-ore. Public enthusiasm exceeded all the bounds of prudence, and Lok, on the crest of the wave, founded the Company of Cathay with the monopoly of all the former rights of the Muscovy Company for trade with Asia by the North West. Within two years it had ended in ruin and disgrace, the gold-ore discredited, the Passage not completed, and the fraudulent share-pushing and loose book-keeping constituting a prototype of the Bubble of 1720. Lok went to jail, although he was not a knave, and Frobisher turned to other adventures.

John Dee—the famous Doctor Dee, whose pursuits of astrology and spiritualism have unjustly overshadowed the reputation due to his great attainments—was a furtherer of all these plans. His influence was important because applied in the highest quarters. His activities were threefold. First, and most public, was that of the mathematician, undoubtedly the foremost mathematician of Tudor England before the rise of Thomas Hariot. Dee made practical use of his talent in devising new methods of navigation for those northern latitudes where the convergence of the meridians and the variations of the compass rendered unsuitable the older practice of the south European masters of the art. He invented instruments and inspired and ex-

---

[1] Quoted in Vilhjalmur Stefansson's edition of *The Three Voyages of Martin Frobisher*, London, 1938, Introduction, p. xcix.

plained new map-projections. He was the instructor of
the chief navigators of his time, and the Muscovy Company thought highly of his training of their captains. It
is easy to decry the work of a theorist who never took a
sight from a rolling deck, but the seamen did acknowledge their debt to him, and John Davis was but the last
of a line of distinguished navigators whom he taught.
There was no public provision for teaching navigation
in England, and Dee devoted his time and money to it
without reward and solely as a patriotic duty. Secondly,
Dee was an intensive student of all the geographical
facts pertaining to the northern passages to Asia. He
desired their discovery, as all thinking men did, for the
benefit which would ensue to his country. He collected
all the records of the past, and maintained touch with
the continental masters of geography. He was persuaded especially of the utility of the North East Passage,
but he welcomed the north-western attempts and also
the project of the South West Passage or Straits of
Magellan. Asia and Terra Australis were his goals,
however reached. In his geographical studies, unlike
his mathematical work, Dee was no publicist. He
moved behind the scenes, writing as little as possible,
but impressing his views by personal conversation upon
the Queen and her ministers and the sea-captains. And
they respected him and were fortified by his learning.
Even Martin Frobisher, that most unbookish of practical men, wrote him a letter of thanks from Shetland,
while on his way to the Arctic ice. What Dee did commit to paper was shown only to the elect. He destroyed
one whole volume as soon as he had written it, and for
the publication of another he refused the considerable
offer of £100. His surviving work reads as though he
feared always that some spy was looking over his
shoulder; for it is allusive and fantastic in phraseology,
and in places so cryptic as to amount to a semi-ciphered

rendering of his thoughts. This was partly because his
knowledge was so exclusive that it really was worth safe-
guarding, and partly because his third and private ambition was ever present in his mind. That ambition
was to establish contact with the culture as well as the
merchandise of the Far East. For in the East he hoped
to disclose philosophical secrets unknown in Europe,
the clues to those occult sciences which fascinated him.
We do not know much of his approach to the occult,
but what we otherwise know of him may assure us that
it was scientific, in an age when such science was not
only difficult but dangerous.

Dee was a valued counsellor of the Duke of Northumberland in his plans for economic salvation, and
was especially the friend and ally of Richard Chancellor, the discoverer of the White Sea. He encouraged
Humphrey Gilbert's north-western plans, and subsequently those of Frobisher, Lok, and Davis. He avoided
the snares of faction, and while candidly wishing well
to those supplanters of the Muscovy Company, he maintained close touch with the Company itself, which he
never ceased to urge and aid to its true work, the discovery of the North East. The abortive voyage of
1580 in that direction was largely of his inspiration.
And, more than this, he condensed and imparted
to the governing circle and the Queen those evidences
of Terra Australis Incognita which Drake was sent to
find in 1577. Some of Dee's most cryptic passages refer
to this design and to his interviews with Hatton and
Walsingham, and even to the scholar's own willingness
to take passage to the South Sea in the *Golden Hind*.[1]

In the late seventies the colonization of North
America came suddenly into prominence as a complement to the Asiatic and Pacific plans of empire-

[1] *Mariner's Mirror*, April, 1929, 'Master John Dee, Drake and the
Straits of Anian', by E. G. R. Taylor.

building. Those plans had drawn their stimulus from the economic depression and social unsettlement of the generation after the dissolution of the monasteries, and in the minds of the projectors the increase of trade had been consciously linked with the relief of unemployment. At the period we have now reached, England began to think that social distress was due to an increase of population which she could no longer support; and direct relief by emigration appeared to be the remedy. For this purpose the Atlantic coast of North America, hitherto neglected, was the obvious region. Gilbert thought of it as a second string to his bow in the North Western effort, and after Frobisher's failure it became the first. In the printed version of the *Discourse* Gilbert wrote: 'Also we might inhabit some part of those countries, and settle there such needy people of our country, which now trouble the commonwealth, and through want here at home are enforced to commit outrageous offences, whereby they are daily consumed with the gallows'; and in 1578, abandoning the immediate search for the Passage, he obtained a patent to take and occupy any part of North America above the latitude of 30 degrees.

Gilbert tried, failed, and died in 1583, but the disaster was only the beginning of new efforts, and his attempt had called forth a greater volume of propaganda than anything that had preceded it. It was for the most part propaganda of the popular and public sort, for there were no geographical secrets to be concealed. Spain indeed might mislike it, but Spaniards did not use the coast in question, nor did their ships frequent the tracks to it; and Elizabeth and Burghley had always been firm for the doctrine of effective occupation as against prescription. Christopher Carleill and Sir George Peckham, associates of Gilbert, both published tracts in 1583 advocating and explaining the colonial schemes.

They held that an American settlement would be a good stepping-stone to the North West Passage and trade with Asia, and to this and the other well-known inducements they added the hope of great sales of cloth to the American natives, and the new attraction of the transfer of England's surplus population. But the Gilbert venture was the occasion of weightier writing than this, for it called forth the first important work of the greatest of Elizabethan publicists, the younger Richard Hakluyt.

Already for several years a Hakluyt had been specializing in commercial geography, the collection and synthesis of facts on the mercantile possibilities of all countries, for the use of investors, scientists, and explorers. This was Richard Hakluyt the elder, barrister of the Middle Temple. The younger Richard Hakluyt, scholar of Christ Church and clerk in holy orders, was his cousin and at first his apprentice in these pursuits. Already the younger Hakluyt was known to Dee and Michael Lok. He had written a pamphlet on the Straits of Magellan, and had brought out an English translation of Jacques Cartier's voyages into the St. Lawrence. He had also corresponded with the great Mercator on the question of the North East Passage, and was recognized as a geographer of standing. The colonization of North America strongly attracted him, and for the rest of his life he was its untiring advocate. He believed that something more than a prospectus was needed for the public education, and in 1582 he published *Divers Voyages touching the Discovery of America*. The volume contained the letters-patent granted by Henry VII to John Cabot, with some other evidences of the early Bristol discovery; the writings of Robert Thorne, then first published; and translations from various foreign authors of passages on the exploration of North America and the waters that might lead to Cathay. It was illustrated by two maps, of which the more important was contributed by Michael Lok, to show in graphic form the discoveries hitherto accomplished. Hakluyt's preface emphasized the necessity for emigration, the good hope of the North West Passage, and the desirability of establishing some public instruction in navigation, to carry on the work in which Dee had been assiduous for thirty years. On this matter Hakluyt had approached Sir Francis Drake, now rich and famous, and Drake had promised twenty pounds a year towards the stipend of a lecturer. A further twenty pounds was needed, and Hakluyt suggested that some nobleman should honour himself by contributing it. Apparently no nobleman did, for Sir Thomas Smith the merchant appears to have found the money; and even then the lectureship was short-lived.

After Gilbert's death Ralegh took up the work of colonization, and in 1584 sent out two captains to make the preliminary reconnaissance of Virginia. Hakluyt worked in his support, and in the same year produced his *Discourse of the Western Planting*, a programme intended, not for the public, but for the Queen. It is a vigorous and comprehensive writing, embodying all the known motives for colonization, and showing that a Virginian colony would strengthen the nation in the approaching war with Spain. That end alone, he thought, the strategical offensive of creating a base in western waters, would justify the Queen in promoting a national effort in America. The Queen, however, left it to Ralegh, and the war began too soon, for it was the concentration upon naval expeditions that blighted the prospects of the young Virginia colony. Hakluyt, like all projectors, underestimated difficulties, more particularly the difficulty of converting gentlemen-adventurers and the unsuccessful poor into industrious and self-reliant colonists. Hakluyt, then and later, was willing to adventure in person. He would

have gone with Gilbert, but was sent instead to Paris
as chaplain to the English ambassador. It was a decision fortunate for him and for English letters; for
Hakluyt, especially in his earlier years, could write. A
brief comparison will illustrate that point. Christopher
Carleill, in his tract above referred to, had quite com-
petently written: 'For who knoweth not, how by the
long peace, happy health, and blessed plentifulness,
wherewith God hath endued this realm, that the people
is so mightily increased . . .', and so forth. The *Western
Planting* gives this in Hakluyt's prose: 'Truth it is that
through our long peace and seldom sickness (two singu-
lar blessings of Almighty God) we are grown more
populous than ever heretofore. . . .' Much of *Western
Planting* resembles this, and there is hardly a poor page
in it. In later life Hakluyt yielded to a mild attack of
euphuism and became at times diffuse, but, even so,
he was never mediocre.

A large part of Hakluyt's work has not been recognized until recent years.[1] It consisted in procuring and
financing translations of foreign books, especially on
America. These were generally published under the
names of the translators, and his own part did not
appear. But his energy was immense and his expenditure considerable. The modest clerical preferments with
which the Queen rewarded him constitute perhaps
the best-justified example of the patronage by which
the state kept public servants in a position to do their
work. It is not possible here to deal further with this
matter, and we must pass to the great book by which
his name is widely known.

While at Paris in the years from 1583 to 1588 he was

[1] The only comprehensive biography is *Richard Hakluyt and the English
Voyages*, by Professor G. B. Parks, New York, 1930. The best text of
Western Planting is in Prof. E. G. R. Taylor's *Original Writings . . . of the
two Richard Hakluyts*, Hakluyt Society, 1935.

able to gain information of many voyages hitherto unknown, and also learned that foreigners had a low
opinion of the English share in exploration. To vindi-
cate the credit of his country and to stimulate it to
further effort he determined to print an exhaustive
collection of 'the worthy acts of our nation' on the sea.
While abroad he obtained much material from French
sources and from Portuguese refugees in France, and
corresponded with people in England and other countries who could help him. He thus accumulated a
pile of manuscripts which in a surprisingly short time
he cast into a coherent book. His work lay not only in
collection but in arrangement, the writing of cogent
prefaces, and the editing of often rough material into
readable form. He extracted it from merchants' letter-
books and seamen's logs, he urged veterans to write him
accounts of their doings, and he personally interviewed
those who could not or would not write; and to all this
he added state papers and printed records from every
source he could find. Much of this was done in Paris,
but a great deal must have been achieved with almost
incredible industry after his return; for in little more than
a year the great book was published, *The Principal Navigations, Voyages and Discoveries of the English Nation, made
by Sea or over Land to the most remote and farthest distant
Quarters of the earth at any time within the compass of these
1500 years*, a quarto volume in black-letter, issued in
1589.

Again it needs close acquaintance to discern Hakluyt's
full share in this performance, which, ostensibly, is for
the most part the work of others. The editor was so
modest that he did not claim credit for much of his
labour. But everyone who reads the adventures is struck
with the fact that their miscellaneous heroes—travellers,
sea-captains, common sailors, humble clerks and craftsmen—were apparently a remarkably well-educated set

of men. There lay the work of Hakluyt. He polished everything and made it presentable while preserving the individual style of the authors. Since bulk had to be kept down, he sometimes omitted unessential passages, and he reduced his own comment to a necessary minimum. To avoid verbiage he had one practice that would be a fault in a modern editor: where he saw errors of fact in a narrative he would correct them without mentioning that the printed result was not what the author had written. But that was the accepted usage of editors. A much larger misrepresentation, and one that has misled modern historians, lies in this: that while he claimed the work to be comprehensive, it was, sometimes deliberately, not so. There were many adventures of his own time, of which he must have heard, which he omitted. These included much that went on in West Africa and Brazil, the whole project of Sir Richard Grenville and his friends for the South Seas, and all but the thinnest accounts of the deeds of Drake. Reasons of state, or at least of expediency, explain most of this. And Hakluyt also was an enthusiast for North America and a northern passage to Asia; other projects made less appeal to him. But the historian needs to be on his guard against the assumption that there is nothing important which is not in Hakluyt; for it is by no means true.

In the next ten years new adventures multiplied and more old ones were rediscovered. Hakluyt therefore brought out a much enlarged version of the *Principal Navigations* in three volumes published in the years 1598–1600. The bulk was more than doubled. The 1589 edition had contained 700,000 words, and to these were now added a million words of new matter. The chief sections enlarged were those dealing with medieval seafaring, North America, and the East Indies, and also there were new narratives of the naval actions of the

Spanish War. As before, the concern with the tropical and South Atlantic and the South Sea was comparatively slight. All modern reprints have been taken from the text of the enlarged edition, and that of 1589 has been little used. It contained, however, certain pieces which Hakluyt did not reprint. One, which he omitted as incredible, was the story of David Ingram, who, by his own account, walked a huge distance over North America in a suspiciously short time, and saw things which no one has ever seen since.

Hakluyt lived till 1616. He was a member of James I's Virginia Company, and the official geographer to the East India Company. He continued to write or finance minor works and collected great numbers of new manuscripts, but he made no further revision of the *Principal Navigations*. At his death the unpublished manuscripts fell to Samuel Purchas, who included some of them with much matter gathered by himself in the huge *Purchas his Pilgrims* of 1625. It is a work of greater bulk than Hakluyt's, but infinitely less readable. The industry of Purchas was immense, but he had no gospel of empire. His interest was in travel for its own sake rather than for its bearing on the national fortunes. In place of Hakluyt's well-written and statesmanlike prefaces and dedications, Purchas describes only his own grievances and difficulties, and he encumbers his text with moralizings and pawky comments. He had little sense of historical values and sometimes cut short important narratives without economizing his own unnecessary remarks. In one tantalizing instance he gives the full text of the address and the subscription of a letter, for their quaintness, but omits all the informative part as too long to print.[1] He helps us to realize Hakluyt's greatness as an editor.

[1] The letter of Albert de Prato to Cardinal Wolsey on John Rut's voyage of 1527, of which we would gladly know more.

But Purchas was Jacobean. The last of the propagandists of the Tudor breed was Sir Walter Ralegh, and his outstanding contribution was different from all others. He left it to Hakluyt to write about Virginia, his first great project, but he was his own publicist for Guiana, the dream of his later life. Here he parted company with Hakluyt, who remained faithful to Virginia and never showed much enthusiasm for Guiana. The word Guiana, as then applied, covered more ground than it does now. It included the whole coast from the delta of the Amazon to that of the Orinoco, and the whole of the upland mass of territory from which some rivers flow northwards to the coast and some southwards to the Amazon. Ralegh was chiefly interested in the uplands, which no European had yet penetrated. He was convinced that there lay the rich and civilized empire of Manoa, ruled by El Dorado, the gilded king. The king's description was transferred to his territory, which became commonly known as the country of Eldorado. The belief in its existence was an outgrowth of the facts and native stories collected by the Spanish conquerors of Peru. Spanish books had told Ralegh of the search for Eldorado in various regions of South America, but the location of the rich state in the Guiana mountains was due to the investigations of the explorer Antonio de Berrío. Berrío's results had not come into print, and Ralegh does not tell us how he became possessed of them. But Ralegh had communication with Spain, even during the war, and had evidently been able to obtain highly confidential intelligence. He believed, on Berrío's authority, that the Orinoco provided the best approach to the difficult highlands.

In 1594 he sent out a pinnace to investigate, and in the following year he went in person, ascending the Orinoco in rowing-boats until the strong currents of the rainy season compelled him to return. He had seen the mountains from afar, and his talk with the river Indians convinced him that Eldorado was there. He at once wrote and published his *Discovery of the Large, Rich and Beautiful Empire of Guiana.*[1] The book is a literary masterpiece, which is and always will be worth reading by those who delight in contact with a brilliant mind. It is also a grand description of a favoured tropical scene. But these aspects were incidental to its purpose, although more purely valuable on that account, and the motive of its writing was in the realm of high politics. The King of Spain, the enemy of England's liberty, and how to beat him—these formed Ralegh's theme. The wealth of the Spanish Indies was the King's weapon: 'It is his Indian gold that endangereth and disturbeth all the nations of Europe.' Many an English expedition had raided the western coasts and picked up comforting crumbs of that vast treasure, but the mass of it came to Spain intact, to pay the armies that might yet enslave England; for the mines of Mexico and Peru were far inland and untouchable by sailors. Now, said Ralegh, we have the certainty of this golden state in the Guiana mountains. We must imitate the Spaniard and go inland to take possession. If we do not, he will: Berrío is hot on the scent, and the King is aiding him. If they take Eldorado, it may well be the final lever to overturn all that England lives for. But if the Queen will move, she may have Eldorado almost for the asking. Its people know the Spanish reputation—Berrío and his set are already committing the usual atrocities on the river folk—and they and the uplanders will gladly receive the Queen's protection and her honest, godly rule. Once occupied, the defence of Eldorado will be easy, for there

[1] The edition by Prof. V. T. Harlow, 1928, has an introduction throwing new light on the explorations of Berrío and their influence upon Ralegh.

is only one way in. And England, with greater wealth than Spain's, and with such men as history has proved, will be preserved, all Europe saved, and the future of the world set right.

Such was the programme, setting no store on gold for private profit, but only for the nation's use. It fell on deaf ears. Ralegh was out of favour, and the Queen was cold. He was unpopular with the great men who could have backed him. Eldorado was not attempted; and we can only regard it as fortunate, for Eldorado was not there. It was the characteristic, perhaps the noble quality, of all these projectors, that their reach exceeded their grasp, and of Ralegh most of all. Yet something remained. Ship after ship, in little nameless expeditions, went out to the Guiana coast, scenting the great prize from afar. Rapids barred access by the rivers, but in their estuaries a trade developed. Then, with the Spanish peace, colonies began, a score of small plantations that failed and are forgotten. But they played their part in history, for they trained the men who colonized the British West Indies. Thomas Warner and his friends, the pioneers of that island dominion, were planters from the Amazon, and they had been led to the Amazon by Captain Roger North, a follower and friend of Ralegh. The Governor of the Amazon Company was Robert Rich, Earl of Warwick, Puritan peer and tropical adventurer. He lived to be Cromwell's colonial adviser, after having himself promoted many Caribbean plantations. Cromwell himself admired Ralegh, and so, with Cromwell's Jamaica, the English Western interest was at length completely founded, not in Ralegh's Guiana, but in the line of his desires.

This brief and hurried sketch of a century of aspiration has left much unsaid. But it may have served to indicate a view of Tudor enterprise that has not been much considered until recent years. The British Em-

pire, indeed, was not founded in a fit of absent-minded-
ness, by third-rate persons who could prosper at no
other undertaking. Its planning occupied the best
brains of thinkers and masters of action. They failed
again and again, but they persisted, and their small
successes were cumulative. And if we think that after
eighty years the success was still negligible, we do them
an injustice. The contrast is great between the petty
oceanic interest of Henry VIII's early years and the
swarm of English shipping when his daughter died,
prying into every coast of the Atlantic, and seeking in
all its four quarters for passage to the Indian Seas and
the Pacific. Much had been done, and much more was
about to be done; and it cannot be denied that the
propagandists had played their part.

IV

THE EASTERN SEAS

THERE are essential differences between the Atlantic and the Indian Seas as fields of European enterprise. In the Atlantic all early voyages outside the home waters of Europe were voyages of discovery, and all the lands and islands west and south were New Found Lands hitherto unknown and unimagined. Their peoples were for the most part savages of little fighting power, and complete European conquest was possible. The aboriginal religions proved unable to hold their own against conquering Christianity. There were rich commodities, but no existent trade in them, and the explorers were able to colonize, and set up governments, and organize commerce comparatively unhindered by any institutions preceding their own. As a result, the American shores of the Atlantic became territorial dominions with dominant white populations, and the surviving natives existed in a very inferior condition.

In the Indian Ocean and the Far East all was different. Long before any European ship sailed those waters, the general layout of their surrounding shores was known. Something was known also of the peoples and the states in which they were organized, and much concerning the commodities which they produced. European travellers of classical and medieval times had collected this knowledge; and after it had been possible for Marco Polo in the thirteenth century to journey through every country from Syria to China and to return in Chinese shipping which visited the chief seaports from Amoy to the Persian Gulf, it is hardly correct to think of Marco's successors in the sixteenth century as the discoverers of Asia. The men of the

Renaissance who found the Cape route to India were indeed African explorers, but, once in the Indian Ocean, they knew what to expect. They were not discovering southern Asia, but approaching it by a new track. The peoples with whom they made contact were much more numerous, more highly organized, and more tenacious of their religious beliefs than any found in America. They were civilized and had no sense of mental or cultural inferiority to the European, although he did very quickly imbue them with a sense of military inferiority. But in spite of that there were no great possibilities of European conquest until comparatively recent times. In commerce again, the eastern process was different from the American. The European did not organize a new trade. He found a vigorous trade permeating the whole area, and he thrust himself into the control of it, but even in his most dominant period he has never carried on the whole of it himself. And so, in sum, the topic we have now to consider is not the founding of a colonial empire in Asia and the maritime enterprise of a colonial population, but the English attainment of a share in the management and profits of a going concern, the Asia of the Asiatics. So stated, it appears less important than the creation of an empire in the Atlantic, but its reactions on English life have been in some respects at least as far-reaching.

The intrusion into Eastern commerce was the original motive of English expansion, but its fulfilment was postponed for a hundred years by the discovery of America. The motive was not forgotten during that period, as the numerous attempts to find a northern passage testify. Sebastian Cabot, Gilbert, Frobisher, Davis, are only the best known among the projectors of the North West Passage; Robert Thorne thought it possible to sail due north across the pole; the Muscovy Company was founded to search for the North East

Passage. None of them succeeded, but the hope survived well into the Stuart period and expired only
temporarily with the voyages of Luke Foxe and Thomas
James in 1631. The Muscovy Company, having experienced the obstacles of the Siberian coast, tried to
develop a land route through Russia to the nearer parts
of Asia. Anthony Jenkinson, travelling in its service,
reached Bokhara in 1558. He found no hope of a
profitable through traffic with the Far East. He then
visited Persia with more promise of success. For several
years the Muscovy factors carried on a Persian trade
by way of the Volga and the Caspian Sea. The profits
and the difficulties were equally great, and the Company withdrew from Persia when that country was
invaded by a Turkish army in 1579. The Turks, who
had levied toll on goods brought from the Persian Gulf
through their own dominions to the Mediterranean,
were naturally hostile to the English attempt to divert
the same trade northwards to Russia. While the Muscovy men were admitting failure other London
merchants were negotiating with the Grand Turk for
access to the East through Syria. The result was the
foundation of the Turkey Company, which became the
Levant Company in 1592, and traded prosperously in
the products of the Near East; but the lucrative commodities of the Far East were beyond its reach. Some
individualist Elizabethans did more. Drake, in his
voyage of circumnavigation, was the first to sail an
English ship across the Pacific and the Indian Ocean.
He laded spices in the Moluccas, and his alleged treaty
with the Sultan of Ternate promised to be the foundation of an English trade. Thomas Cavendish made a
similar voyage with different ports of call, and obtained
much information on the prospects of trade with China.
John Newbery travelled overland to India, but disappeared on his way home. Ralph Fitch, his com-

panion, wandered on to Burma and Malaya, and returned in 1591, after one of the most arduous journeys on record, to describe the gorgeous prospects of southern Asia, but to report also that an overland trade with it was not feasible.

Meanwhile, during the whole of this century in which the English hankering after an Eastern trade was so apparent, the Portuguese had been successfully conducting one by the only frequented route, the South East Passage round the Cape of Good Hope. The question therefore arises why, until the last decade of the century, England refrained from the only certain method of accomplishing her desires. The superficial explanation is that the English respected the Portuguese rights by the papal donation and prior discovery, but it does not carry conviction. Henry VII, in his patent to the Bristol men in 1502, had clearly stated that he would respect effective occupation and nothing else, while his patronage of John Cabot had shown that the papal donation meant nothing to him. These precedents were not forgotten, and were the basis of every project of the Tudor period. With regard to Portugal the Tudor sovereigns were particularly unsparing in their interpretation of oceanic rights. Henry VIII encouraged William Hawkins to trade with Guinea and Brazil, and Elizabeth backed her Gold Coast traders to the point of irregular warfare. If Englishmen had sent ships round the Cape they would have found numerous Asiatic ports where they could colourably have alleged that the Portuguese were not in effective occupation. The reasons for their abstention were therefore not based upon amity and submission to the doctrine of prescription.

During the first half of the sixteenth century the prime deterrent was undoubtedly lack of knowledge. The English captain of the period did not know how to sail a ship round the world; neither his geography nor his navigation were equal to the risk of the capital investment involved. Even the comparatively short adventures in the Atlantic at that time were nearly all under the guidance of foreign pilots. Presumably no Portuguese navigator for the East could be tempted to serve, and the Portuguese would permit no educated Englishman to sail with them and learn their secrets. In 1541 the English government asked that some of its merchants might be allowed to accompany the next navigation to Calicut to buy spices for English consumption, but the request was refused. By comparison the northern passage appeared easier, provided only that it existed; for, measured on the globe, it was very much shorter, and most of it would consist of coasting the northern shores of Asia or America with frequent halts for supplies.

After 1550 England began to produce competent navigators of her own—Richard Chancellor may stand as the first of the new type—while her knowledge of geography was immeasurably extended by the labours of such men as Dee, Eden, and the Hakluyts. But still the reluctance to adventure by the Cape continued, and hopes were centred on a northern passage. An economic motive was undoubtedly operative. While the buying and selling of tropical spices was known to be lucrative, the urgent need during the mid-Tudor depression was to sell English cloth; and cloth would find its market in cold and temperate climates. The inhabitants of northern Asia and northern America, whose purchasing powers were grossly over-estimated, would finance the opening of the northern passages to the Spice Islands. The supposed certainty of a cloth trade added to the speculative possibility of the spice trade was an attraction offered only by the northern passages. Fluid capital was scanty, as is shown by the very small sums actually invested in such good business as the Gold Coast provided; and England simply had not enough to embark on the sole chance of dealing in spices at the end of a voyage of 16,000 miles. The Grenville syndicate of 1574 indeed proposed to take the long way by the Straits of Magellan to their speculative goal of Terra Australis Incognita, but they had wayside financing in their minds in the form of plundering Peru; and Drake showed most brilliantly how it could be done. The Cape route was devoid of this attraction; the gold of South Africa lay yet unsuspected beneath its soil.

But above all else there was a shipping difficulty, and not until it had been solved could Englishmen invade the Indian Ocean in force. The difficulty was that the ships of those days required large crews in proportion to their size, and that the stowage of victuals for so many mouths for a long voyage left insufficient space for cargo. But it was found that very large ships suffered proportionately less from this disability than small ones, and the working rule became that the longer the voyage the bigger must be the merchantman to carry a profit-able lading. The Portuguese had worked the Guinea coast with small caravels, but they had no sooner found their way to India than they began to build huge car-racks of twelve and fifteen hundred tons. A ship of this size did not require six or seven times as many men as a two-hundred tonner, and thus she could devote less space to stores and more to cargo. The economic reason was the sole reason for building big ships for long voyages. They were no safer than small ships, and in some circumstances less safe. In the open ocean it was quality rather than bulk that yielded safety, and in coastal waters the great ship was at a disadvantage, being more likely to be wrecked in getting into port. Portugal, with her ocean frontage, bold coast-line, and the deep water of the Tagus estuary, could become an owner of great ships, while England was still a land of little ships. English merchants seldom built ships of over two hundred tons, of little value for the Eastern trade. And so this dilemma hindered Tudor enterprise by the Cape, that there were no ships suitable to begin it, and that until success was assured it would not pay to build ships that would be useless for any other trade. By the close of the century the difficulty was decreasing. Private men were building larger vessels to take part in the war with Spain, while increasing experience of ocean work was rendering it possible to cut down the numbers of the crews. Only when this process had advanced was it feasible for the English to make the Cape passage to the East.

Apart from the question of the route, there were two distinct policies for the foundation of an English interest in the East Indies. In 1580 Philip II had forcibly occupied Portugal in pursuance of his claim to the throne. By so doing he had offended Portuguese patriotism, which hoped for an ultimate restoration of independence under the Pretender, Don Antonio, a refugee sheltering alternately in England and France. The anti-Spanish sentiment was especially strong among the officers of the Portuguese colonies, including those of the Far East. Thomas Cavendish had been assured in Java that if Don Antonio would come out there he would have the East Indies at his disposal. Drake was always a believer in the utility of Don Antonio as an instrument of English policy, and it may be said that the Devon men in general followed Drake's opinion that the best method of entry into the Eastern seas would be for the English to appear as restorers of Portuguese liberty, and to be rewarded by a share in the Portuguese monopoly. There are indications that this was the secret intention of Richard Hawkins, the son of Sir John Hawkins, who sailed from Plymouth for the Far East in 1593: we have hints that on his return the time would be ripe for the launching of a great plan of empire in which the Queen would be interested— in plain words, a Devon East India Company. But Richard Hawkins never reached the East. He sailed by the Straits of Magellan and sought to plunder the Peruvian coast by the way. There he was rounded up and captured by the superior forces which Spain had by this time stationed on the coast.

Meanwhile the Londoners were working on a different plan. From 1585 England was at war with Philip II and therefore with his Portuguese subjects. The direct method was thus to attack and supplant the Portuguese in their Asiatic possessions. The scarcity of capital available for a risky venture made it necessary in either plan to secure plunder while the new trade was being established. The Devon men looked to Peru for this purpose, and so they sailed by the Straits of Magellan. The London men decided that the best way was by the Cape, and determined to finance their venture by capturing Portuguese ships in the East. They were greatly encouraged in 1587, when Drake took a homeward-bound carrack at the Azores. Her lading was fantastically valuable, and her papers revealed many secrets of the trade. Soon after the defeat of the Armada an East Indian expedition was planned, and in 1591 it actually took shape under the leadership of George Raymond and James Lancaster. They touched at the Cape and then entered the Indian Ocean. Raymond was lost at sea, but Lancaster reached Malaya. He captured a number of ships, some laden by the Portuguese and others by native merchants, and these latter he was careful to release. Lancaster's voyage would have been a brilliant success but for one circumstance, that he was losing men by disease so fast that it was doubtful if he would be able to work his ship home.

In fact he could not do so. His crew was so weak on the homeward voyage that he had to seek refreshment in the West Indies, with 24 survivors out of the 97 with whom he had entered the Indian Ocean. While he was ashore collecting victuals, the ship drifted off with only six men on board, and was taken by the Spaniards. Lancaster was brought home by a French privateer - who befriended him, and all his booty was lost. The next Eastern voyage, under Benjamin Wood in 1596, was even more disastrous, for only one man is known to have survived, a French sailor who was rescued by a Dutch ship after living in Crusoe fashion on the then desert island of Mauritius.[1]

In spite of the risks the potential profits made an irresistible appeal. Another carrack was taken in 1592, with an even richer lading than that of 1587. The Dutchman Linschoten, who had managed to travel East with the Portuguese, published a description of what he had seen, and Richard Hakluyt had his book translated for English information. The Dutch themselves began a regular series of voyages from 1595 onwards, and John Davis took service in one of them to learn the navigation. At length all obstacles were overcome and the Londoners formed the East India Company, which dispatched its first expedition in 1601 with James Lancaster and John Davis in charge. For this venture the members of the Company raised a joint stock of £68,000. Forty-eight years previously the Muscovy Company, intending also a voyage to the Far East, had subscribed only £6,000. There had been a considerable rise of prices in the interim, but after allowing for that, we have still an illustration of the

[1] For the voyages of Lancaster and Wood, and other early expeditions to the East, see Sir W. Foster, *England's Quest of Eastern Trade*, London, 1933, *passim*. Other recent authorities on the Elizabethan period are cited in the present writer's *Age of Drake*, London, 1938.

effect of half a century of ocean trade and privateering upon the fluid wealth of London; for at either date the subscription represented the utmost of which the City was capable.

Thus, in the opening year of the seventeenth century, England began her continuous effort to gather the riches of the East. The arena in which she was to play her part had already been exploited for a hundred years by the Portuguese, and here it is convenient to draw attention to its salient features, physical and economic. The Indian Ocean, unlike the Atlantic, was one-sided. Its northern shore swept in a rough semi-circle from East Africa round by southern Asia to Malaya and the great south-eastern archipelago which contained the Spice Islands. The semicircle was completed by the coast of Western Australia. The Portuguese may have already discovered Australia by 1530, but, if so, they had concealed the fact from public knowledge, and it was left for the Dutch to rediscover it in the early seventeenth century. The southern limit of the ocean was unknown, although generally supposed to be bordered by an antarctic continent reaching well into the temperate zone. The wind system of the Indian Ocean was of vital importance to all its navigators, whether for commerce or war. North of the equator the north-east monsoon, equivalent to the north-east trades of the Atlantic, prevailed roughly for the winter half of the year; but in the other six months the direction was reversed and the monsoon blew from the south-west towards the heated area of southern Asia. Although there was a period of uncertain winds at each change of the monsoon, the average tendency was sufficiently steady to render west-to-east navigation alone possible during the summer and east-to-west in the winter. South of the equator the south-east trades prevailed throughout the year as in the South Atlantic, and farther south still, in the parallels beyond the Cape of Good Hope, was the belt of strong west winds which blow in the open ocean right round the world. On the coasts of China and Cochin-China the monsoon system was experienced, but in the great archipelago between China and Australia the winds were local and variable. The equator cuts the middle of the archipelago, and the effect of the islands is to break up the great air-currents prevailing in unobstructed waters.

From remote antiquity the maritime business of southern Asia had depended on the monsoons. Their effect was to make Arabia the commanding position during one half of the year, and the coasts of Malaya during the other half. Midway between them jutted out the Indian peninsula, whose ports, besides con-ducting the trade of India itself, formed places of refuge for traffic that could not complete its voyage before the change of monsoon, and thus early developed into entrepôts deliberately used for exchange between East and West. The monsoons rendered the use of the Indian ports also seasonal. Most of them were open roadsteads without shelter from an on-shore wind, and thus the south-west or Malabar Coast of India was safe and active during the north-east monsoon, while the Coro-mandel Coast, facing the Bay of Bengal, was similarly useful during the south-west monsoon. Southern India was chiefly desirable to strangers for its entrepôt busi-ness. The great plains of northern India, on the other hand, were a rich producing area coincident with the effective extent of the Mogul Empire, whose commerce passed mainly through the port of Surat on the west, and through the Ganges basin eastward into the Bay of Bengal.

Owing to the great variety of soils, climates, and peoples existing from East Africa to China and Japan it was natural that there should be a vigorous inter-Asiatic trade in the locally produced luxuries of every

country. But, more important to history, there existed
a trade between Europe and Asia, dating certainly
from the period of Roman civilization. Southern Asia
could supply the luxuries that Europe demanded.
Europe on her side produced few goods that Asia
needed, saving only silver. Asia was deficient in silver-
mines, while Europe had a small supply, and the puls-
ing commerce of all the Eastern seas required as large
a quantity of silver currency as it could attract. Gold
was less prominent as currency, since it had a luxury
value of its own for the making of beautiful decora-
tions; and gold was less used as coin than as a material
bought with silver coin. The governing factor of inter-
continental trade until some time after the advent
of Europeans to the Indian Ocean was the amount
of silver that Europe could find for the purchase of
Eastern goods. After the mid-sixteenth century, when
the silver-stream began to flow from Mexico and Peru,
the quantity was greatly increased. The capital investment of 1601, to which allusion has already been made,
eleven times as great as that of 1553, is mainly an index
of the effect of Spanish silver upon the trading capacity
of London merchants.

For many centuries the Arabs of the Red Sea and the
Persian Gulf dominated the inter-continental trade.
As men of business they were perhaps not the equals of
the Indians and the Chinese, and indeed it was common
for Arab merchants to employ Hindu clerks and factors.
But the Arabs had the mentality of a ruling race; they
excelled in initiative and active courage, they were
bold and intelligent explorers, and they were unsur-
passed as seamen and designers of ships. Only when
they were opposed to Europeans who shared all these
qualities did their one great defect prove fatal, that
they were incapable of discipline. On the Asiatic world
they worked their will. From their home ports they

monopolized the trade with Surat and the entrepôts of southern India, and thence they worked eastwards to Malaya and through the straits to the Spice Islands and China. Everywhere the local shipping fed them as tributaries, and every ounce of sea-borne goods from the East to Europe passed through their hands.

Then came Vasco da Gama to Calicut in 1498, and within a dozen years the monopoly had changed hands. The Portuguese were not discoverers. They knew the conditions and were ready with their plan: to seize the Indian entrepôts, to challenge Arab sea-power to a decisive issue, to seal up the exits from the Red Sea and the Persian Gulf, and then to occupy the Straits of Malacca, the gateway to the lands of silk and spices. Thus the Portuguese empire of the East was founded, not a land empire, but the most purely maritime dominion that the world has seen. On land its flag flew over seaports only, all the way round from the East African coast to the archipelago and to Macao in the Canton River. Even so, it was only a few of the ports that were occupied and governed. The rest were dominated by the prestige of visiting ships. The Portuguese never attempted to carry on the whole trade of the ocean themselves. They canalized the cream of it for the Cape passage to Europe, but the vast majority of ships and merchants within the area remained Asiatic. It was a process for collecting the maximum of profit with the minimum of men. The men were always the difficulty, for Portugal was a small nation, and the majority of her sons who sailed East never came back. Chiefly for manning purposes, and to relieve the drain upon the homeland, she planted colonists at Goa, the Indian head-quarters, in order to breed soldiers and mariners upon the spot. But the Goanese stock quickly deteriorated, and the experiment failed.[1]

[1] For the Portuguese effort up to and including Vasco da Gama, see

Portugal held the monopoly for a hundred years, and then lost it to the English and the Dutch almost as rapidly as she had taken it from the Arabs. There were intelligible reasons why the new-comers gained ascendancy. The Portuguese trade from India to Europe was conducted on behalf of the Crown by officials who were its salaried servants. At such a distance they could not be efficiently controlled, and they gave more energy to illicit private business than to the service of the state. Exactly the same effect was to be seen in the eighteenth century in the great days of the English and French East India Companies, which were also the declining days of the Dutch East India Company: in every case the Company remained poor while its servants grew rich. The process entailed a moral deterioration which was especially notable among the Portuguese, who quickly lost that supreme devotion to duty observable in the conquering pioneers of the first generation. Then also Portugal suffered badly when she fell under the rule of Spain in 1580. Spaniards knew and cared little about the Asiatic business, and used Portuguese resources for their own purposes. Portugal did not regain independence until after 1640, by which time the Eastern empire was lost. But, most of all, the Portuguese decline was due to lack of men. The small home population could not support the casualties of empire. Negroes had to be employed in the fields of Portugal itself. The national stock, at first a splendid west-European type, was diluted and lost its dominating qualities, and even so its numbers decreased. The Portuguese, after a century of empire, were far from being the men of the Renaissance who had set forth to explore and conquer.

The English and the Dutch both sought to exploit

E. Prestage, *The Portuguese Pioneers*, London, 1933. The later record may be read in K. G. Jayne, *Vasco da Gama and his Successors*, London, 1910.

the whole trading area, and at first showed no inclina-
tion to restrict themselves to particular regions. Both
desired the Spice Islands and the trade with China and
Japan, and both were interested in India and Persia.
Unlike the Portuguese, the new-comers applied their
greatest energies to the archipelago, not only because
the spice trade was the most immediately lucrative, but
because a development of navigation rendered the
islands more accessible. The Portuguese had simply
copied from the Arabs the practice of monsoon sailing.
After passing the Cape they had coasted East Africa
until they came into the monsoon belt north of Zanzibar
and Mombasa, and thenceforward kept north of the
equator until they entered the Far Eastern seas by the
Straits of Malacca. Thus their movements swung to
and fro in six-monthly alternations, and the entrepôt
coast of India was their natural strategic centre and
head-quarters. But the great archipelago had a better
means of access than this. Java and the greater part of
Sumatra were south of the equator on the edge of the
south-east trades; and southward still was the zone of
the westerly winds. Within a few years the Dutch and
some of the English ships were following an entirely
novel route. From the Cape they ran before the west
wind in the latitude of 40 degrees or more until they
had made the longitude of Java. Then they turned
north across the trades and passed into the archipelago
by the Straits of Sunda, between Java and Sumatra.
Coming home, they kept in the trade-wind belt until
they drew near to Africa, and then rounded the Cape
in the manner of the Portuguese. The new route was
quicker for the Far East and also independent of the
seasonal delay of the monsoons. It is hardly possible
that the Portuguese had not thought of it, and very
likely that they had tried it. But running for weeks
before the strong gales and mighty seas of the 'roaring

forties' demanded good ships. Perhaps the carracks were not equal to it. We know little of their design and their sailing qualities, but the indications are that seaworthiness may have been sacrificed to bulk and stowage.[1] The Dutch soon evolved East Indiamen fit for the conditions of the southern track. One result of following it was that they discovered Western Australia, and several Dutch captains painfully learned the dangers of its coast by being wrecked upon it through overrunning the longitude from the Cape. At least one English ship left her bones upon a reef in this neighbourhood, and the Trial Rocks, long marked upon the charts, commemorated the name of the unlucky vessel.

Until the Restoration the English East India trade was in an experimental condition and the subject of numerous fluctuations of policy. The traditional outline of its story is that the Company sought primarily to establish itself in the archipelago and was beaten out of that desirable region by the Dutch, after which it turned its chief attention to India as a second and less attractive choice. Further, it has often been said that the trade was very prosperous until the interest in the Spice Islands was lost, but then fell on bad times and suffered severe losses until a new period of prosperity was inaugurated by Cromwell's reorganization of the Company in 1657, confirmed by Charles II in 1661. While there is some truth in this view, it is by no means the whole truth, and a consideration of some circumstances that have often been denied their due prominence leads to a considerable shifting of the emphasis of the story as a whole.

[1] Since this was written, the suggestion has received support from an article describing a reform in the building of Portuguese Indiamen in 1622. The carracks or *naós* before that date are said to have been deficient in sailing quality, seaworthiness and fighting power. (*Mariner's Mirror*, October, 1940, 'Admiral Corte-Real and the Construction of Portuguese East Indiamen', by Capt. C. R. Boxer.)

At the outset the most immediately profitable trade to the investors was that of the spices—the pepper obtainable in Sumatra and Java, and the cloves, nutmegs, and mace of the Moluccas. But to the national interest this trade appeared less beneficial because the spice regions offered little market for English manufactures, and none for the woollen cloth which was the most important of all. In the popular view of finance and economics it was prejudicial for the nation to buy spices with silver coin, and so, whenever there was a depression in general trade, the Company's critics cried out against its export of silver. For this reason, if for no other, the Company had to seek business in the more populous mainland of Asia, where it might be able to sell some manufactured goods. Then again it was not possible for the spice trade to yield high profit together with continuous expansion. The market for spices in Europe was limited. So long as the supply was well below the limit of demand the prices were high and the profits enormous, but the limit was soon reached at which it became disadvantageous to increase the volume of trade, for the market was glutted and prices fell. The same process was observable at the same period in another luxury trade, the tobacco industry of the Atlantic colonies, where a few years of intensive exploitation produced a glut that forced the West Indian plantations altogether out of the business. In the Spice Islands the Dutch early perceived the danger of overdoing the trade. They fought the English for the monopoly and went far towards achieving it, but they were then compelled to maintain prices by destroying plantations and severely limiting the output. Their success was decisive but restricted, and in the long course of events their stationary spice monopoly became less and less important in relation to the expansion of world trade, and even to the other trades of the Eastern seas. In fact the Dutch applied their greatest effort of empire-building to an object that was only temporarily worth attaining. The slow but progressive decline of Dutch national power after the middle of the seventeenth century was due to many causes, but one of them was undoubtedly this misapplication of energy in the East.

The financial record of English trade in the East corrects the impression that Dutch aggressiveness did it decisive injury. Up to the period of the defeat in the Spice Islands, towards the end of James I's reign, the East India Company's profits were large, but after that period, and right on through all the troublous times to the Restoration, profit remained considerable; and no investor in all the various capital stocks of sixty years ever lost his principal or went without an ultimate dividend, saving only the adventurers in the small expedition of 1608, when both the ships concerned were lost at sea. Apart from that the worst result attained was that of the Second Joint Stock of 1617. When it was wound up in 1633, the investors received the return of their capital together with $12\frac{1}{2}$ per cent. This was certainly a poor return for so long a period, but, as will be seen, the failure was not solely due to the victory of the Dutch. Subsequent stocks subscribed from 1628 to 1650 yielded return of capital together with dividends ranging from 34 to 121 per cent. obtained after considerably shorter periods.[1] The English Company indeed was paying larger dividends than the Dutch during the years in which they were trading in competition in the Spice Islands; for the English had no fortified factories, and their resident merchants were scattered in small parties in places where they lived

[1] The Company's finances for this period are carefully explained, and the statistics collected, in W. R. Scott's *Joint Stock Companies to 1720*, 3 vols., Cambridge, 1910.

under native jurisdiction. The Dutch, on the other hand, exercised the self-denial to cut their dividends and devote some of their gains to strengthening the business by establishing forts, garrisons, and fighting squadrons. The massacre of Amboyna remains one of the most atrocious crimes in history, but the exclusive policy of which it was the expression was not altogether unjustified in view of the respective sacrifices of the two companies.

Statistics show that the English investors on the whole did well, and never after 1608 suffered a loss of capital. That being so, why were they so frequently in distress, full of forebodings for the future, and threatening to withdraw from the whole enterprise? The answer lies partly in their own chaotic methods of administration, and partly in the indefensible behaviour of English governments. Until 1657 there was never a permanent joint-stock of capital upon which the management could operate a long-term policy. For the first twelve years every voyage was a separate financial undertaking, separately wound up as soon as possible after its conclusion. Different groups of the Company's members were therefore competing in the markets against one another, and there was in effect not one great company but several small ones, for the annual expeditions took years to buy and sell their cargoes and therefore overlapped. The overhead expenditure also, on Asiatic factories, presents, and embassies, was common to all and difficult to apportion. After 1613 the separate voyages gave place for a time to terminable joint-stocks subscribed for a limited term of years, but even these overlapped and the confusion continued. In times of uncertainty, also, the members would not subscribe even for a limited term of years, and there were occasional reversions to the single-voyage system. The Company as a whole was thus in a chronic state of internal dissension, and while the subscribers to a given stock were quietly pocketing their dividends public attention was diverted to the clamours of a succeeding group who were still in the throes of uncertainty. These evils were very wasteful and remained incurable until the principle of a permanent, non-returnable stock was adopted.

During the same sixty years the public regarded the East India investors as selfish profiteers who were monopolizing and mismanaging what should have been a national business. Merchants who had not been admitted to the Company were determined to ruin it, ostensibly in the name of fair play for all, but really in order to succeed to the monopoly. A dishonest form of propaganda therefore denounced the East Indian trade as economically unsound, a drain on the country's wealth, and a waste of ships and men needed for the national defence; and at the same time demanded that this pernicious enterprise should be thrown open to all comers.

All this may be regarded as natural mercantile vigour, and in sum a healthy process. But nothing can be said for the statesmanship of the early Stuart governments. Having established the Company they should have supported it or ended it on fair terms. In practice they gave it nominal support and continually undermined it. James I allowed the interloper Sir Edward Michelborne to sail to the East and commit piracies for which the Company paid the smart; and having, as King of England, given exclusive privilege to the English Company, proceeded as King of Scotland to charter a rival body who were not even bona-fide traders but blackmailed the English into buying them out. When the Company, entirely by its own enterprise and resources, captured Hormuz in 1622 and opened up the Persian Gulf, the Lord Admiral (Buckingham) was allowed to claim £10,000 as his perquisite from the booty, while the Crown took a similar amount. To make a levy on the winnings of privateers in waters where the might of the Royal Navy alone made their operations possible was just; but to do so in the East, where the Company alone bore all the expense of maintaining the national interest, was very unjust. Charles I carried on these crooked practices. He had behaved badly to the merchant Sir William Courteen by expropriating him in favour of a courtier from the ownership of a colony in Barbados planted entirely at Courteen's expense. Courteen had lost £10,000, and a few years later Charles compensated him at the expense of the East India Company. In 1635 the Company, having by its own efforts defeated the Portuguese in a prolonged war, obtained a local peace in the Convention of Goa, whereby English ships were allowed to trade at the Portuguese stations. Charles I immediately licensed Courteen and a group of courtiers to trade in the Eastern seas at any places where the Company had hitherto not been doing business. The Courteen Association sent ships to Portuguese seaports in western India, and also to Macao in China, to reap the fruits of the Company's success. Owing to bad management and ill-luck the Courteen ventures failed to yield a profit, and the Association degenerated into practices which brought the national name into contempt among Asiatics who did not distinguish the one English group from the other. It robbed native shipping and circulated quantities of base coin. Sir William Courteen, an honourable man, had died before this took place, but his associates, in spite of all their villainy, had ultimately to be bought out by the Company. This was not the only instance of damage wrought upon the Company by the unkingly shifts of Charles I, and it may truly be said that it suffered as badly from him as from the Dutch.[1]

If the Company at home was always insecure, it laid firm foundations in the East. Although it was excluded after 1623 from the Moluccas, the true Spice Islands, it continued to obtain the pepper of Sumatra, and maintained its factory at Bantam in Java until 1682. But, as we have seen, the spice trade had no great future, and long before the struggle with the Dutch became acute the Company was wisely turning its attention to the trades of the mainland which were capable of almost unlimited expansion. India, and particularly northern India, produced three classes of goods which Europe could absorb in almost any quantity available. These were cotton cloths of various sorts, calicoes, chintzes, and muslins, plain and printed; indigo; and saltpetre.

Cotton fabrics, besides serving for ornament, supplied the growing demand of European civilization for washable underclothing. Hitherto European linen had been the only supply, and linen was so expensive as to be available only to the well-to-do. Indian cotton was much cheaper. Its import not only satisfied but stimulated a demand. It strengthened England's commercial position by enabling her to sell to her neighbours what she had previously been buying from them. And slowly but incalculably it contributed to the social equalization of modern times by permitting the poor man to share the personal cleanliness of the rich. The cotton import from India continued to be of prime

[1] The general record is told in Sir W. W. Hunter's *History of British India*, vol. i, London, 1899. The *Cambridge History of India* deals only with India proper, and its concise treatment seems disproportionately brief. See also two articles by Sir W. Foster in *English Historical Review*, vols. xix and xxvii. The naval history of the struggle between English, Portuguese, and Dutch is related in a series of articles in *The Mariner's Mirror*, beginning in vol. x (April, 1924), by Admiral G. A. Ballard.

importance to the national economy until the early
years of the nineteenth century, when the machines of
Lancashire suddenly reversed the process and under-
sold the Indian hand-weaver in his own country. Yet
another century, and the Indian mechanized himself,
with results temporarily unfavourable to ourselves of
this generation. The whole sequence was set going
when Thomas Aldworth settled in 1612 at the head of
the English factory of Surat.

The chief industry of England was the making of
woollen cloth. As soon as the import of cotton became
extensive the cloth-makers complained of unfair competition, and in the late Stuart period began to press for
restrictive legislation, even to the burying of the dead
in woollen shrouds. But the public demand was too
well established, and Indian cottons were never completely excluded. India, however, aided the English
cloth-weaver with a dyestuff of better quality than he
had hitherto used. The American tropics yielded dye-
woods producing red and yellow tints, and Mexico
exported cochineal; but blue had been extracted from
the woad plant, and the disadvantage had been that
its colour was impermanent. The indigo of India
was a rich and fast dye that became indispensable
to the makers of good cloth, and the demand kept
ahead of the supply. The West Indian planters grew
indigo, but could not compete in quality with the
East Indians.

Saltpetre provided an obviously expanding trade, for
it was a constituent of gunpowder. European supplies
were scanty and of low quality, and the progress of the
military art would have been seriously hampered had
not Bengal come to the rescue with saltpetre of ample
quantity and excellence. As the musketeer drove the
pikeman from the fields of Europe, and the maritime
powers built ships-of-war in growing numbers, armed

them with guns of increasing calibre, and fought them with an energy unknown in the sixteenth century, the indispensability of India was realized. However other trades might fluctuate, there was hardly ever a time from the Defenestration of Prague to the fall of Napoleon when a cargo of saltpetre would fail to arrive on a rising market. These were the solid elements of the Company's success on the Indian mainland.

From Surat the English ships found their way into the Persian Gulf, whose control they wrested from the Portuguese by the victory of Hormuz. Raw silk in considerable bulk, in addition to textiles, was the reward of this enterprise. At first the silk was sold to France, but by the close of the seventeenth century a silk industry was well established in London. Another secondary import was the coffee of Mocha, which suddenly became a fashionable drink at the time of the Restoration. Tea came a generation later. Englishmen in the East were drinking it before James I was dead, and the Dutch brought small quantities to Europe before the middle of the century. In England it did not seriously compete with coffee until the reign of Anne, although it is notable that Samuel Pepys drank his first cup in the Restoration year.[1] But tea, although a slow starter, had a mighty future, and was destined to provide the greatest of all the expanding trades of Asia. The purchase of tea entailed intercourse, direct or indirect, with China, until modern times the only producer.

Before the seventeenth century ended the Company had established trade and factories in every useful area from the Red Sea to the coast of China. The conventional enumeration of Surat, Bombay, Madras, and Calcutta is misleading, for there were many other stations, each with its handful of English factors, not

[1] *Diary*, Sept. 25, 1660.

only in the archipelago, but in Arabia, in Persia, on both coasts and in the interior of India, in Siam and Tonkin, in Japan, and even tentatively in the exclusive ports of China. Many of these factories were short-lived, but their abandonment did not always imply the loss of the trade done in them. Japan was early given up, never having yielded profitable business: the Cipango of Marco Polo proved on acquaintance to be the most illusory tale of hearsay inherited from the medieval past. The Moluccas were lost to the Dutch. But elsewhere trade expanded, although factories might disappear. The agency at Mocha, for example, was discontinued because it proved more economical to receive the coffee from Arab dhows at Surat. Bantam, after the decline of the spice trade, was useful as an entrepôt for the cargoes transferred from Chinese junks, and was given up to the Dutch in 1682 when direct contact with China was being developed. Tonkin was also a feeler towards China, with little attraction for its own sake. On a small map it appears that the Dutch consolidation in the archipelago should have barred access for English ships to the China Seas. But this was not so. The Dutch took Malacca from Portugal in 1641, but its mere possession did not command the Straits, any more than that of Batavia commanded the Straits of Sunda. In the absence of fighting squadrons rivals could always pass through; and in the latter half of the century the fighting squadrons were increasingly absent; the slow Dutch decline had set in. The obstacle to English progress in China was not the Dutch, but the Chinese, whose favours could be wooed only by the greatest tact and experience.

The abandonment of English factories was largely due to a change in the Company's policy when it was reorganized by Cromwell and Charles II. During its first half-century it sought to be the primary collector of its own cargoes by carrying on various local trades in order to feed the larger factories that laded its ships for London. The adventurers in the Second Joint Stock (1617) sent out eighteen small vessels which were intended to remain in Asiatic waters for this purpose, which also accounts for the multiplicity of little factories so frequently founded and relinquished. The early establishments on the Coromandel Coast and in Bengal were for this trade, sending cotton goods to Bantam to exchange for spices and Chinese produce; and the Convention of Goa in 1635 allowed the opening of a local trade from Surat southwards to the Portuguese stations on the Malabar Coast. Experience showed that it was unprofitable for the Company to operate local trade routes. They were the natural business of the highly efficient Asiatic shipping, and a management far away in London could not compete successfully. Moreover, the Company's servants in India, extremely ill paid if they made nothing beyond their nominal salaries, came to regard the local trades as their own perquisite. They were soon investing in and managing what were called 'the country ships', and the Company could not prevent it. During the Civil War and the Commonwealth the Company's affairs at home fell into confusion and uncertainty, and its servants in the East were left in doubt of the outcome. They supported themselves by engaging in the local trades exactly as if they had been Asiatic merchants, and their prestige and experience enabled them to hold their own against the guilefulness of the East. Some of them broke connexion with the Company's service and lived independently. The wrecks of the Courteen Association also left a sprinkling of unattached adventurers in Asia, as did the numerous interlopers of the Commonwealth period. From about 1640 onwards right through subsequent history we find numbers of private Englishmen making their living in all the ports of southern Asia. The great majority were obscure and unrecorded,[1] but casual mention of them occurs continually in travellers' narratives. That very significant term 'the country ships', always cropping up, accounts for a great part of their activities.

In 1661, therefore, the reorganized East India Company admitted the situation and withdrew from the port-to-port trade. In so doing it concentrated its staffs into a few central factories, shipping goods to England, and saved the expense of maintaining a number of small ones. Its regular liners making the Cape passage were fed by the country ships which were not under its management.

The Restoration period was a time of great prosperity for the Company, which enjoyed unwonted government support from Charles II and his brother. The Dutch Wars, and particularly the last, of 1672, occasioned some local losses, but on a broad view were really advantageous. The great exertions of the Dutch, in repelling the armies of Louis XIV from their soil in a six years' struggle, debilitated both them and their enemy; and England, which withdrew from the last war after two years, profited in all the fields of commercial enterprise, including the oceanic trades. At home the Company's prospects were again clouded by the Revolution of 1688, whose consequences enabled the interlopers to form a new and rival East India Company. But the inherent strength of the old Company was good even against government hostility, and the result was the fusion of 1709, which produced the United East India Company, destined to weather all storms for a hundred and fifty years.

[1] A notable exception is Samuel White, whose career is recorded in most interesting detail in *Siamese White*, by Maurice Collis, Penguin Books, 1936.

Until the days of Clive, in the mid-eighteenth century, the United Company carried on its business ostensibly on the lines laid down at the Restoration. But the beginnings of a gradual shift of emphasis are to be noted, and this change proceeded much more rapidly after the great territorial conquests which ensued from the struggle with the French. Briefly, what took place was that the individuals composing the Company—its directors, shareholders, and servants—became more important than the Company regarded as a corporation. Dividends remained steady, but not sensational; and the dividends represented only a small proportion of the profits made. Even the shareholders began to care less about the interest they received than about the influence and patronage they could exercise. The salaries paid by the Company had always been low, and private trade had been a necessary emolument. In the eighteenth century the private trade began to rival the importance of the Company's trade. The captains and senior officers of the ships were allowed stowage for their own goods, made large profit out of the passengers, and enjoyed other perquisites. The staffs of the factories were merchants on their own account, sold goods to the Company, and served it in their spare time. Of all the young men who went out to the East only a minority lived to come home in middle age, and these select survivors were quite determined to come home rich. The Company in England acquiesced, and shareholders and directors troubled less about efficiency than about nominating their relatives to places in the Eastern gamble, or selling their influence for political favours, indirect payments of all kinds and, occasionally, for hard cash. In effect the joint-stock organization of the East India trade became a cover beneath which a privileged brotherhood carried on business for individual profit, as in the regulated companies of the past.[1] The total amount of wealth thus controlled by what was known as East India patronage was very great. It was a considerable agency in the social and industrial changes of the eighteenth century; and, if fully mobilized in support of a political party, it was capable of influencing the course of history. George III feared in 1783 that his obnoxious ministers meant to entrench themselves permanently in power by seizing the East India patronage; and hence came his extraordinary measures to defeat Fox's India Bill and the strong support he received in a quite unconstitutional method of achieving his purpose. Eastern enterprise had indeed grown mightily in the two centuries since Drake had paid the first English visit to the Spice Islands.

[1] This development is the theme of *Trade in the Eastern Seas, 1793–1813*, by C. N. Parkinson, Cambridge, 1937.

V

THE NATIONAL INTEREST IN OCEANIC
ENTERPRISE

IN the Tudor period the leaders of thought discussed oceanic enterprise, clarified policy, and presented the results to the public so effectively that they formed an accepted body of doctrine. The England of the Stuarts took for granted a great deal of this doctrine, put it into practice, and elaborated it in gaining further experience. In some respects the change of dynasty in 1603 hardly involved the opening of a new period, for continuity was more evident than innovation. What change took place was in essence the change from war to peace, and for most of our purposes it produced, not new departures, but a resumption of the activities interrupted in 1585.

Before dealing with that resumption a result of the war may be mentioned. It left the national consciousness strongly affected by the glamour of the wealth to be won by warlike expeditions on the ocean. Drake pre-eminently, but many others in addition, had gained great plunder by comparatively trifling outlay, and Drake had possessed a magnetic quality, a flair for publicity, which had impressed his achievements on the public memory to a greater extent than can be accounted for by the rather meagre published records of what he had done. Drake had made every man talk of him, and the tradition outlived his own generation; and down to the middle of the eighteenth century a war with Spain had for the generality an attraction such as no other war could offer, for it called up legends of booty easily won from Spanish incompetence, and righteously won from torturers of Protestants and oppressors of the Indians. In 1626, when Charles I half-heartedly challenged Spain, a London publisher printed *Sir Francis Drake Reviv'd*, purporting to be the hero's own account of Nombre de Dios and the capture of the gold-train; and was sufficiently encouraged by the sales to reprint it two years later and to follow it by *The World Encompassed*, the story of the great oceanic raid which had ballasted the *Golden Hind* with treasure. The same appeal recurs in Thomas Gage's book *A New Survey of the West Indias*, of 1648, reprinted in 1655 when Cromwell had launched his Western Design to conquer the tropical wealth of Spain. There the ease of conquest was prominent, the rottenness of the apparently mighty power; and it was Gage who attractively termed it 'a Colossus stuffed with clouts'. In the early eighteenth century any dispute with Spain produced a crop of pamphleteering on the same lines, that Spanish weakness and Spanish cruelty were ordained for the just enrichment of Englishmen; and Jenkins' Ear marks a well-known culmination of the argument. No sooner was war declared than Drake became topical, and Johnson contributed a short life of him to the *Gentleman's Magazine*, while Anson was preparing in practice a new version of *The World Encompassed*. The righteousness of the Elizabethans remained still a part of English religion in Kingsley's time and produced a last romantic echo in Tennyson's *Revenge*.

The colonization interrupted by the Spanish War began again with vigour on the signature of peace. The idea was still generally held that emigration was necessary to relieve the over-population of England. The last years of Elizabeth had indeed been a hard time on account of taxation, the interruption of trade, and some bad harvests, while the profits of privateering had begun to fall off. With the peace, trade revived rapidly, and financial statistics show that under the early Stuarts the wealth of England increased at a much greater rate than its population.[1] Yet the wealth fell to the more enterprising, and observers were impressed with the prevalent distress. As late as 1623 the economist Misselden could write, 'I am persuaded that there were never more people, never less employment.' In 1609 a supporter of colonization had spoken of 'the swarms of idle persons . . . having no means of labour to relieve their misery', and had declared, 'it is most profitable for our state to rid our multitudes of such as lie at home, pestering the land with pestilence and penury'.[2] In the same period there are other similar statements on record, echoes, in effect, of the Elizabethan doctrine of Gilbert and Hakluyt. Colonization as a remedy became once more what it had been in the 1580's, an agreed policy.

Mercantile considerations dominated in deciding the question where to plant the colonies. Those who influenced policy were not mainly the emigrants themselves, but the governing circle and the investors who were to finance the operation, 'purse adventurers' as contrasted with personal adventurers. The old idea that the natives of America would prove to be large purchasers of English cloth had faded, and colonies were expected to be chiefly valuable as sources of supply of those commodities which England herself could not produce. England was buying her naval stores, wines, fruits, linens, silks, and many other luxuries from European countries, and it was held that every such purchase drained the national wealth and enriched rivals. If England could extend herself into

[1] W. R. Scott's *Joint Stock Companies*, vol. i, gives a general survey of successive good and bad periods in English economic life.

[2] G. L. Beer, *Origins of the British Colonial System*, New York, 1907, pp. 36, 39.

climates where her own people could produce such things, a clear economic gain was expected. An English empire might be rid of the curse of unemployment and at the same time self-sufficient, while selling its surplus wares to rivals from whom it bought nothing, and so draining their wealth into its own coffers. The choice of sites for colonies was therefore not mainly dictated by considerations of where an English community could most healthily seat itself and live the English life. That was left to be the much later ideal of the settlers of Australia and New Zealand. The Jacobean promoters looked first to what the colonists could produce for sale, a motive which most commonly involved their living an un-English life in an exotic climate.

One important commodity, however, pointed to the cooler parts of North America as a desirable region, and that was naval stores. Dependence on the Baltic for masts, plank, hemp, and pitch was considered not only economically unsound but strategically dangerous, for the Navy might be starved by some turn of European politics. Newfoundland, Nova Scotia, and Maine thus had a colonial attraction, and the Stuart governments sought to promote settlements which should export naval stores. On the whole, the attempt was a failure, simply because it proved to yield no immediate profit. To establish a lumber trade able to compete with the Baltic producers would have been a lengthy business needing state expenditure, and the private investor was not attracted. When, later on, the New England colonies, founded for quite other reasons, did produce naval materials, they used them to build ships of their own and compete with Old England in the Atlantic trades; and throughout the old colonial period the English Empire never was self-sufficing in this respect.

All other considerations of supply demanded colonies in climates which should be warmer than that of the British Isles. Ralegh's Virginia, whose attractions were known to all from the accounts printed by Hakluyt, was the scene of the greatest effort of the new time. It was expected to lead to some western approach to Asia, and also to produce the commodities then being bought from France and Spain. All the expectations failed, and Virginia found grace in the colonial scheme only by growing tobacco, a commodity which had not entered into the calculations of the promoters. Tobacco as a substitute was very reluctantly accepted by English statesmanship. James I was not alone in thinking that it was a harmful and disgraceful trade, and it was some time before conservative opinion was consoled by extensive sales of the poison to the Dutch and other foreigners. Tobacco, however, proved too strong for its critics. All Europe took it up with zest, and it served as the economic foundation of the English colonial empire both in North America and the West Indies. Tobacco was also the principal product of the numerous plantations founded in Guiana and in the Amazon delta under James I and Charles I, although other tropical commodities, such as dyestuffs, rare woods, and cotton, were there prominent. In the second generation in the West Indies sugar displaced tobacco, while the Guiana enterprises were discontinued. Thus, by the middle of the seventeenth century, the supply-colonies were Virginia, Bermuda, and Maryland, producing tobacco, and the Caribbean Islands, growing mainly sugar, together with some cotton and dyestuffs.

New England, sturdiest of all the colonial groups in character and corporate stability, does not fit the above statement of the economic policy followed in Stuart colonization. The reason is that the founders of New England were not moved by economic policy but by religion. Moreover, New England was not a deliberately but an accidentally selected site. The Pilgrim Fathers, so called,[1] who founded the pioneer settlement of Plymouth, were members of a Nonconformist sect who desired to get away from Europe in order to practise their religious ideas in seclusion. As poor men they were prepared to work for their living, but they had no clearly determined views of the sort of work they would do; they would adapt themselves to any country which, on religious grounds, should seem desirable. In 1619 the leaders were inclined to choose Guiana, whose plantation products then seemed so attractive, as the scene of operations. Had this handful of obscure men, less than two hundred strong, persisted in their choice, the history of the world would have been changed, for New England, as we know it, would not have come into being. On second thoughts, however, the Pilgrims rejected Guiana, not because the tropical life seemed unsuitable, but because the English planters there were continually involved in fighting with Spaniards and Portuguese, and the Pilgrims desired to live in peace with all men. They then obtained permission to settle in unoccupied territory belonging to the Virginia Company, and sailed with that purpose in 1620. Their ship made her landfall at Cape Cod, well to the northward of the intended destination, late in the year, when a coasting voyage down to Virginia would have been dangerous. Only then did they make their decision to settle near Cape Cod,

[1] The pioneers of Plymouth never styled themselves the Pilgrim Fathers, nor were they so described by their contemporaries. The name is first traceable in 1799, when it was applied to all the early New Englanders. It began to be limited to the Plymouth men in the mid-nineteenth century. Its romantic flavour is quite out of character with the reality.

and so to begin without premeditation the occupation of New England.

'Plymouth Plantation', as its pioneers named it, proved in the succeeding years to be a region where English farmers and villagers could practise the same agricultural pursuits as in the old country, with freedom from the old country's social restrictions, and above all, with the opportunity to engraft upon a sober English way of life the Calvinist organization of church and state. Other Puritan malcontents in England observed this and realized that here was a promised land, a New English Canaan, to which Calvinists might withdraw in force, to preserve all that they valued in their old life and to reject all that they found intolerable. And so the great exodus to New England set in with the establishment of the Massachusetts Bay Company in 1629 under the leadership of John Winthrop. It was Winthrop and his associates who were the real founders of New England as a community with a great place in history. The Pilgrim Fathers of Plymouth had been content with quiet obscurity, thankful to escape notice, and desiring to cut no great figure in the world. The Massachusetts leaders were men of higher social rank, not satisfied with toleration, but filled with a passion for building and ruling, and creating a Calvinist state for all the world to see. They took with them their farm servants and personal dependants, and accepted the swarm of ordinary emigrants of no deep religious colouring who were then ready to leave the mother country in quest of a prosperity greater than they could look for at home. The rulers of New England put them in the way of that prosperity, each man according to his worth, and exacted in return as strict a conformity to Calvinism as Charles I was demanding to his conception of the Church of England. There was nothing democratic in early New England. A strong-willed oligarchy of English squires dominated an unenfranchised mass for the good of their souls, and the mass took religion as they found it and prospered in the economic freedom of a new country governed on sound business principles. In its early conception New England was not a colony of supply but a colony of subsistence. In that character it succeeded so rapidly that it soon had a surplus of foodstuffs for export. With them it began to supply, not Old England, which did not need them, but the West Indian plantations which concentrated upon tropical crops. Thus began the merchant-shipping interest of Boston, and its speedily developed carrying trade in plantation produce. Boston ships were soon working the trade routes round the whole Atlantic circle, much to the annoyance of London, by whose investments and for whose benefit the plantations had been founded.

New England was thus from the outset an exception, not only in the obvious matter of religion, but in the economic scheme upon which the colonies in general were being developed. She successfully maintained her exceptional position and evaded conformity to the general principles of colonial regulation which we have now to consider.

It is necessary to be clear upon the aims which were quite consciously pursued by the founders of the old colonial empire. They desired to increase the prestige of the nation by extending its dominions. They believed that well-established colonies in the West would be useful naval bases for a war against Spain, a means by which cruising squadrons would be enabled to operate against the plate-fleets, 'a bit in the ancient enemy's mouth', to use an oft-quoted phrase which originated with Sir Thomas Dale, an early governor of Virginia. They hoped that emigration would relieve social distress at home. They calculated that the national wealth would be increased by the production in the colonies of goods hitherto purchased from foreigners; by the profits ensuing to the mother country from the colonial trade, and especially from the resale of surplus commodities to the continent of Europe; and by the revenue which the Crown would derive from customs duties. They looked for a further increase of wealth, at a later stage when the colonies should have grown populous, by the sale of manufactures and foodstuffs to them: the colony as a market would follow on the development of the colony as a source of supply. And finally they held that the colonial trade would make the nation more powerful by increasing its shipping, its mariners, its stock of naval materials, its dockyards and shipwrights. Another motive was often mentioned in prospectuses but seldom received attention in practice, the propagation of the gospel by the conversion of the heathen.

All of the above motives are to be found in the propaganda of the Elizabethans. They were not all equally prominent during the whole course of subsequent development. Fashions in emphasis varied, and sometimes one and sometimes another incentive took first place. It is to be noted that some of them involved a diversion rather than a creation of trade. The soundness of procuring goods at a greater cost of transit from the other side of the Atlantic rather than from the ports of northern Europe would have appeared questionable to economists of the nineteenth century. It was not so to those of the seventeenth. To them the employment of English shipping outweighed questions of cost, and the longer the voyage the better they were pleased. To carry goods three thousand miles employed more ships and seamen than to carry them three hundred; and the oceanic trade, the trade of long voyages, was deliberately preferred. The reason for this may be misunderstood. The motive for desiring a great mercantile marine lay less in the ships themselves than in the men. Even in the early Stuart period the time had passed when the armed merchantman could play a useful part in a fighting fleet, although she was still employed for that purpose, with unsatisfactory results, until the campaigns of Blake. In war the merchant ships had become more of a liability than an asset to the Navy. But the merchant seamen were indispensable. The state could afford no regular naval personnel in time of peace, and at the outbreak of war it had to enlist thousands of seamen from that part of the mercantile marine which found itself in home ports. The same reasoning applied to the great numbers of shipwrights kept in employment by the long-distance trades, and to the stocks of material for their use; they were an inexpensive reserve available for the naval dockyards.

One advantage of colonization already mentioned, the sale of foodstuffs to plantation colonies, draws attention to the fact that English agriculture was then generally sufficient for the needs of the home population. In order to preserve that condition and to allow a margin for bad seasons, an export of victuals in normal times was thought valuable. The sending of corn and salt meat, butter and cheese, to the plantations employed English husbandmen in excess of the usual need, and created a reserve for emergencies.

The regulation of the tobacco trade illustrates the motives of colonial policy. When tobacco became fashionable it was discovered that it could be profitably grown in southern England. In a short time an extensive culture developed, and then both James I and Charles I prohibited it firmly. Their reasons were, first, that English soil ought to be growing necessaries

and not a luxury; secondly, that tobacco-growing in
the colonies provided employment for surplus men who
were not needed in the fields at home; and thirdly,
that colonial-grown tobacco could be taxed at the
customs houses, whereas no mechanism as yet existed
for collecting an excise on the home-grown product.
In the conditions of the time, this reasoning was un-
exceptionable, and the prohibition of home-grown
tobacco was probably the soundest piece of mercantile
policy enforced by the early Stuart governments.

To achieve the full advantages of the colonial trade,
it was necessary to regulate it. It was not sufficient to
rely upon the natural preference of colonists for trading
with their own country. The Dutch were becoming
the greatest mercantile power in the world, and their
ships were ubiquitous. No sooner was Virginia producing tobacco than Dutchmen were there buying it,
and the Dutch on the whole did more business with the
Guiana plantations than did their English founders.
The Stuart governments early took alarm at this and
sought to check it by a series of regulations. The
restrictions were not embodied in Acts of Parliament
until the Commonwealth. Both James and Charles
held that trade regulation pertained to the royal
prerogative, which they exercised by Orders in Council. The two kings did not show much concern for the
promotion of English shipping. They were interested
in the social aspect of colonization, and still more in its
financial aspect. They continually anticipated revenue
by accepting lump sums from capitalists for the rights
of future collection, and the farmers of the customs
were quick to complain when cargoes from the colonies
failed to pass through English ports. It is to their
influence that much of the royal activity must be
ascribed.

In 1621 the Council sent orders to Virginia to ship

its tobacco exclusively to England, and four years later the rule was extended to the other colonies. But nothing was said about using English ships, and the Dutch remained free to carry the trade. When the Caribbean colonies began to take shape, they were placed in 1629 under the proprietorship of the Earl of Carlisle, and one of his privileges was the collection of all duties on the islands' trade, whether payable in English ports or in the islands. He cannot be described as the farmer of these duties, since he paid nothing for them, but his interests were parallel to those of the farmers. Together they kept the matter before the Council, of which Carlisle himself was a member, and persistent efforts were made to enforce the English destination of all colonial cargoes. Bonds were exacted from colonial shippers, the money to be forfeited if their goods were not brought to England; and, to facilitate supervision, London was made the sole port of entry for tobacco. This not proving sufficient, Charles I in the 1630's established a naval patrol in the Channel, with orders to stop all incoming ships from the colonies and place men on board to ensure that they were navigated to London. Finally, in 1636, Charles ordered that tobacco was not to be shipped in foreign bottoms, and the policy embodied in the later Navigation Acts was at length outlined.[1]

Not only was the policy outlined, but the resistance to it, which became traditional in later days, was early afoot. The payment of a duty in England increased the cost of tobacco which was intended for an ultimate continental destination, and the English colonists were competing against those of other nations. The English duty on goods for the European market therefore came out of their pockets, and they were determined to

[1] In addition to G. L. Beer, op. cit., see the present writer's *Caribbee Islands under the Proprietary Patents*, Oxford, 1926, pp. 96–101.

evade it. They did so by various methods, and the Stuart regulations were largely ineffective. It became usual for the Virginians to trade with the Dutch in defiance of the King's orders. They had no need to defy the King's ships, for neither James I nor Charles I ever sent a single cruiser across the Atlantic. As for the West Indians, their resentment at the proprietary tyrannies of the Earl of Carlisle was so great that they were in a condition of smothered war with him and his officers, and the Dutch appeared in the guise of friends.

It must be said that the attempt to staple the tobacco trade in England was only one aspect of the policy. The other was that colonial tobacco was given the monopoly of the English market. Not only was tobacco-growing in England forbidden, but foreign-grown tobacco was virtually excluded by very heavy duties. For example, in 1632, while Virginia tobacco paid fourpence per pound, foreign-grown tobacco was charged two shillings, and very little was imported. The colonists were glad to have the English monopoly, but did not see why they should not trade elsewhere as well. The arrangement was not one-sided, but they had never willingly entered into it.

The early Stuart attempt to regulate the colonial trade broke down with the opening of the Civil War in 1642. The colonists, however Royalist they might be in sentiment, refused to obey any trade regulations by King or Parliament, realizing that neither side had any force to spare for compulsion. Thus for ten years the colonial trade was open, and the Dutch grasped an increasing share of it, until at length the Commonwealth found opportunity to assert its authority.

During the abeyance of the central authority the Parliamentary leaders thought much on colonial policy, although they were unable to act. Among these leaders were the Earl of Warwick, whose influence had ensured the adhesion of the Navy to the Parliamentary cause, and who had in the past taken the lead in several colonial schemes; and John Pym and Oliver Cromwell, who had been members of the Providence Island Company, which had planted a Puritan settlement in the Caribbean. Parliament drew much of its support from the wealth of London, and the London merchants were growing concerned at the advance of the Dutch. So successful did Dutch intrusion become that it seemed hardly an exaggeration to say that the English had founded an Atlantic empire only for the Dutch to enjoy the fruits of it.

The question came to a head immediately after the death of Charles I. The new Commonwealth appointed a committee to report on the colonies and their trade, and how best that trade might be made useful to England. On that point the instructions were quite uncompromising: the interests of the mother country were to be the sole consideration, and there was no mention of the interests of the colonists. Shortly afterwards a revolt broke out in the plantation colonies, which realized that the victory of Parliament would entail the revival of trade restrictions. The victory of the King, had it occurred, would have entailed the same thing, and the plantations would then in all probability have resisted him. As it was, they proclaimed their Royalism, recognized Charles II, and defied the Commonwealth. This course was taken by Virginia, Maryland, Barbados, and Antigua, while the other island-colonies waited to see the result. Of the four rebel colonies Barbados was the richest and most populous. Its area was about that of the Isle of Wight, but to the Barbadians their revolt did not appear preposterous. They could turn out as many men in arms as had won the Battle of Naseby, and they had no fear of England's sea-power. The Navy had never shown its flag across the Atlantic since the colonies had been founded, and there seemed no reason to expect that it ever would.

The Commonwealth answered with the Navigation Act of October 1650, a measure distinct from, and fully as important as, the better-known Act of 1651. The Act of 1650 was first emphasized and explained as a fundamental step in British policy by the late George Louis Beer, some thirty years ago. But Beer's work[1] is read mainly by specialists in colonial history, and his discovery, for such it may be called, has hardly yet passed into the general body of knowledge. It amounts to this, that while the Act was ostensibly framed as a temporary measure to cope with a rebellion, it contained nevertheless some clauses which were designedly so worded as to be of permanent effect, continuing in operation after the rebellion should have been put down. Briefly summarized, the Act of 1650 prohibited all trade with the four rebellious colonies for the duration of the rebellion; and also, in a clause inconspicuously worded, prohibited trade by foreign vessels with any of the colonies, whether in rebellion or not, and without any provision that the enactment should end with the rebellion. In fact the prohibition of foreign intercourse with the colonies continued to be enforced by the Interregnum governments, to the best of their ability, right up to the Restoration of 1660, when the measure was absorbed into the new Navigation Act passed in that year. The more famous Commonwealth Act of 1651, often wrongly described as Cromwell's Navigation Act, dealt with foreign commerce in general, and not with the colonies, and is sufficiently well known not to need description here. Although Cromwell was interested in colonial affairs,

---

[1] *Origins of British Colonial Policy*, New York, 1907.

and most likely approved of both of these Acts, there is no evidence that he had any hand in promoting them, for he was on active service at the material times. The Act of 1650 was completed a month after the Battle of Dunbar, and that of 1651 shortly after the Battle of Worcester, and during their inception and passage Cromwell was absent from Parliament.

In effect the Commonwealth statesmen laid the foundation of the legal restrictions on colonial trade which continued to be the basis of policy throughout the life of the old colonial empire. They did so in conscious pursuance of principles that were to remain active during the same period, that the colonies must contribute to England's wealth and also, by employing shipping, to England's power, which in return would defend the colonies. The preamble to the Act of 1650 says that the colonies 'were planted at the cost and settled by the people . . . of this nation', and 'are and ought to be subordinate to and dependent upon England'. The preamble to the Act of 1651 is brief and pregnant: 'For the increase of the shipping and encouragement of the navigation of this nation, which, under the good providence and protection of God, is so great a means of the welfare and safety of this Commonwealth, be it enacted . . .' As is well known, the authors of these statements were not content with words, and were already hard at work strengthening the Navy. In 1651 they dispatched a squadron to the West, the first in the half-century since Elizabeth had died. This force dealt first with Barbados, which it reduced by a bloodless blockade after seizing all the Dutch merchantmen found trading there in contravention of the Act of 1650. A smaller detachment entered Chesapeake Bay and paralysed all recalcitrant traffic, whereupon Virginia and Maryland could only submit. Antigua did the same without awaiting treatment. Then followed a hard-fought naval war with the Dutch in 1652–4. Its causes were complex, but its chief result was to compel the enemy to admit the validity of the Navigation Acts.

Cromwell became Protector while the war was in progress, and was able to enjoy the fruits of the Commonwealth policy while following ideas peculiar to himself. The Commonwealth, inspired by the immediate interests of mercantile London, had set itself to drive out the Dutch intruders from England's Atlantic trade. Cromwell, in religious and oceanic outlook, was Elizabethan. He intended to complete the Elizabethan tasks which, in his view, the Stuart kings had shamefully laid aside. To him the Dutch were natural allies, as in the days of the Armada, against the Catholic sea-powers. He had dreams of what an Anglo-Dutch alliance should do, in partitioning the whole oceanic enterprise of the world by the line of the Pope's meridian—Brazil and all the East to the Dutch, the Caribbean and all the rest of America to the English. But the scheme was too vast to be practical, and the peace of 1654 failed to produce friendship, much less alliance. Cromwell then took up his campaign alone. From Portugal he got what he wanted without trouble. Her oceanic ascendancy had decayed, and at home she was still struggling to obtain Spanish recognition of her independence. By the treaty signed in 1654 Cromwell obtained from John IV what Drake had hoped from Don Antonio: freedom for Englishmen from the attentions of the Inquisition, and rights to trade in West Africa, Brazil, and the East. In practice those rights developed almost into an inheritance of the dying Portuguese empire. Without a moment's pause the Protector turned to Spain with similar demands: freedom from the Inquisition, and free navigation in the Caribbean. But Spain refused compliance, and Cromwell attacked her without declaring war.

Cromwell's Western Design, the undertaking to conquer the whole Spanish colonial empire, was an almost complete failure. It achieved only the capture of Jamaica, a virtually derelict island with only a few hundred Spanish colonists. Cromwell's miscalculation was due to the false ideas then prevailing among Englishmen about the strength of Spain. Thomas Gage, the author of *The New Survey of the West Indias*, had stated in that book that the American empire was so rotten that it would fall to pieces at a touch, and Colonel Thomas Modyford, an experienced planter of Barbados, had advised the Protector to the same effect. With Royalists and European ill-wishers to be faced at home, the Protector could not send his veteran troops across the Atlantic. He provided a scratch force without discipline or experience and dispatched it to a failure which was long regarded with shame. In Gardiner's words, Cromwell gathered a mob and styled it an army; and a mistake so remarkable in the creator of the New Model shows how much English statesmanship had yet to learn about the conditions of Atlantic empire-building.

In the course of a generation Jamaica developed into a valuable colony, but its interest to the subject of this lecture is greater than that; for Jamaica provides a clear illustration of views which were then taking shape about Atlantic colonization, and which continued to influence the course of events for the next hundred years. By Cromwell's time, not only had the stream of voluntary emigration out of England ceased to flow, but the conviction that emigration was socially necessary had ceased to be held. No longer was it said that the country was over-populated. On the contrary, economists were beginning to believe that a growing population was desirable. The people were now regarded, not as the consumers of a fixed stock of necessaries, as in a blockaded city, but as the producers of goods whose sale would bring wealth: the more people, the more trade, and the more wealth and national power. Therefore, the emigration of useful citizens was not advocated by publicists in the later seventeenth century, nor in the eighteenth. But there were citizens who were not useful: political and religious dissidents, and all the numerous offenders whose crimes merited the death penalty. These might very well be sent to the colonies, though their emigration would not be voluntary. This reasoning, moreover, was English, and not British. The associated realms of Scotland and Ireland were regarded by English mercantilists as rival countries, not as parts of their own state. Thus there was no objection to promoting the emigration of Irishmen and Scots, for that would mean the weakening of rivals and the relative strengthening of England. Emigration policy had therefore become that of encouraging and even enforcing the exile of undesirables but of retaining all well-behaved and industrious inhabitants.

For the complement of this doctrine we must look to the colonies. They were now valued almost exclusively as producers of trade-goods for the employment of English shipping and the enrichment of English merchants; which meant that the plantation colonies were highly valued, and the New England colonies not at all, for New England was by this time employing its own shipping to the enrichment of its own merchants. It was obvious that the more people there were in the plantation colonies the greater would be their output of trade-goods, and so mercantile policy sought to increase the plantation population by every means except the emigration of good Englishmen from home.

It was ready to fill the plantations with British undesirables, with any New Englanders who could be
induced to move south, and even with foreigners from
the continent of Europe. The Commonwealth sent
out to Barbados the prisoners-of-war taken by Cromwell
in Ireland, Scotland, and at Worcester; but after
Worcester there was peace in the British Isles, and
Cromwell as Protector had to use other expedients.

The prospective conquests of his Western Design
made the problem pressing, and even the one actual
conquest of Jamaica taxed his ingenuity. The poor
quality of his expeditionary force has already been
mentioned, together with the fact that he could not
afford to part with his good troops. Some of these
latter might have been spared for a short campaign,
but that was not in Cromwell's mind. The men of his
Western expedition were not intended to come back.
They were first to conquer Spanish territory and then
to settle down as its colonists. He therefore composed
the force of English undesirables—a few men drafted
out of each of his regular regiments, whose colonels
naturally picked the worst and most troublesome
soldiers, and civilian wastrels impressed from the slums
of London. These worthless wretches were set to
colonize Jamaica. They made a hopeless mess of the
task, and in a year or two were nearly all dead. When
this result was becoming apparent, Cromwell tried
very hard to induce New Englanders to go to Jamaica,
since they were undesirables so long as they lived in
New England, although as Jamaica planters they
might be very useful. His blandishments failed. New
England was fully conscious of being a metropolis in
the imperial trading system, and its inhabitants had
no intention of taking a step downwards to become
tropical labourers exploited by others. Only then did
Cromwell turn to the solution that was obvious on

purely local considerations. He threw open Jamaica to the experienced colonists of the Lesser Antilles, and they, after a hard struggle, made it a successful plantation. But it was somewhat disappointing to the mercantilists of London, since it involved only a transference but no net increase of their Caribbean population. There is of course no evidence that Cromwell personally originated these policies. He had neither the temperament nor the time for economic reasoning. But he certainly acted on the advice of a group of London merchants who devoted close attention to the problems of Atlantic trade.

The principles of emigration discernible in the Jamaica business continued permanently in force. Cromwell himself induced a few Norwegians to go to Antigua, a promising but backward island. After the Restoration the Carolinas were founded with high hopes of producing the commodities of France and southern Europe. The promoters tried to obtain French colonists in order to introduce vines and silk-worms, but not many Frenchmen actually settled. Some New Englanders did re-emigrate to South Carolina, which was in accordance with the general policy, but the other pioneers were chiefly Barbadians, and few emigrants went out directly from England. At a later date a small but energetic Scottish element settled in the colony. At the opening of the second Dutch War an English force captured New Amsterdam in 1664. It had about 7,000 Dutch inhabitants, nearly all of whom were retained as subjects of the English crown. The colony, renamed New York, was not of the plantation type, but was nevertheless regarded more favourably than New England, for two reasons. First, its strategic position rendered its tenure essential to an efficient enforcement of the Navigation Acts, which was the motive for its acquisition; and secondly, the valley of the Hudson led inland to country in which quantities of beaver and other furs could be had from the Indians and sold at a profit in Europe, like the plantation products. New York was therefore held to be in need of emigrants, and to the Dutch nucleus were added Quakers and Catholics from England and Ireland, and Huguenots from France after the Revocation of the Edict of Nantes, a good example of the cosmopolitan type of colonial population created by the unwillingness to send out normal, law-abiding Englishmen. New Jersey and Pennsylvania, peopled partly by Quakers, and to some extent by Germans and Swiss, were also illustrations of the same policy.

The West Indies were a more difficult and more urgent problem. The expansion of the sugar industry depended upon an increased supply of manual labour, and the conditions were such that voluntary emigrants, whether foreigners or English, could not be obtained; for there was now very little chance for the poor man to rise to prosperity on the highly capitalized sugar estates. Emigration had thus to be enforced. Under Charles II it became customary to reprieve a large proportion of the criminals who incurred a death sentence, and send them out to work for the planters, as slaves in all but the name; and the eighteenth century continued the practice, although in that period the usual destination was in the southern American colonies. Rebels were similarly dealt with, among them the Scottish Covenanters and the unfortunates of the Monmouth rebellion, some hundreds of whom were rescued from Kirke and Jeffreys and consigned to bondage in Barbados and Jamaica.

But all these expedients were insufficient for the labour needs of the West Indies and of South Carolina and Virginia, and increasing resort was made to the negro slave. Before the Civil War there were very few negroes in the plantations. During the ten years of unrestricted Dutch intercourse they grew more numerous, for the Dutchmen had seized many good stations in West Africa and were able to supply slaves at attractive prices. The Commonwealth Navigation Acts, backed by naval strength, restricted the Dutch business, but there was no alternative supply, for English slaving was yet undeveloped. After the Restoration the matter was taken in hand. Charles II chartered the Royal Adventurers to Africa, and later the Royal African Company, and the flood of black labour set in, to increase without intermission until the abolition of the trade in 1807. The chartered traders had a nominal monopoly of the slave trade. But in practice, owing to the great extent of the African slaving coast, they could not enforce it. Interlopers abounded from the outset, and before the middle of the eighteenth century they had fairly swamped the chartered monopoly. The equipment of slavers and the import of slave-grown sugar and tobacco made the merchants of Bristol rich, and the preparation of the raw products for the market employed her population. Later in the eighteenth century Liverpool likewise prospered on the slave-trade and slave-grown cotton, while the fortunes thus accumulated were available for investment in the mills of Lancashire.

In sum, the emigration policy of the mercantile empire[1] was successful in providing hands to create plantation products. But it was successful at the expense of making a colonial population of dubious quality and loyalty. The southern slave-owners and their slaves were not, and could not be, a strong limb of the nation. The middle colonies of America were cosmopolitan. The New Englanders, of pure English descent, were ceasing to be colonists at all, in the sense

[1] See *Cambridge History of the British Empire*, vol. i, ch. vii.

in which mercantilism used the word; they were rather the rivals of old England in the business of exploiting the colonies. A really healthy empire population could have been produced only by a steady emigration of normal, contented Englishmen, carrying their self-respect across the Atlantic. After 1689 there were no more religious exiles, and the typical emigrant from England was the transported criminal. Established Americans viewed him with distaste and insensibly regarded him as a fair sample of the home population. Home-staying Englishmen, knowing the kind of man they were sending to the colonies, came to think of him as a typical colonist, and set down all colonists as an inferior race accordingly. Mutual contempt had much to do with the restiveness of the Americans under George III.

In tracing the history of the emigration policy initiated under Cromwell we have run on beyond the important Restoration period, which is notable for its work in other aspects of the same process, the confirming of England as an oceanic power. For that was the essence of the whole effort. From the mid-seventeenth century onwards, sea power was a primary object of all English governments; and the oceanic branch of it, being capable of unlimited expansion, received more attention than the short-distance trades with European countries, which economists were inclined to view as comparatively stationary in volume. The social advantages once expected from colonization were now little thought of. Colonies and a colonial population were desired because they would produce long-distance trade and employ ships and men. The increase of national wealth would support a fighting Navy, and the merchant seamen would man it in time of war. A strong Navy would not only defend the colonial possessions but would secure respect and advantages for English trade in all the waters of Europe, and by virtue of its ubiquitous pressure would obtain for England that rank as a first-class power which her continental neighbours were obliged to seek by means of their armies. Such was the doctrine that had been taking shape for a hundred years past. By 1660 it was complete and unquestioned.

Charles II and his advisers accepted it with enthusiasm. The Commonwealth Navigation Acts were held to be invalid, as was all other legislation that had received no royal assent. But the new government lost no time in replacing them by a measure which embodied all their provisions, and more. The new Navigation Act of 1660 allowed foreign ships to bring to England nothing but the produce of their own countries, all indirectly transported stuff having to be brought in English ships. It reserved the trade between one English port and another (the coasting trade) to English shipping. It made regulations discriminating heavily in favour of English-caught fish. All this was substantially a repetition of the law of 1651. As regarded the colonies, the Act repeated that of 1650, by prohibiting foreign intercourse with them. It went further, by enumerating all the chief plantation products and commanding that they should be sent only to England or to other colonies. This was a revival and a great extension of the stapling policy of James I and Charles I, which those kings had applied only to tobacco. Lastly, the Act defined an English ship as one both built and owned in England, Ireland, or the colonies, and manned by a crew of whom at least 75 per cent. were English, Irish, or colonials. The Commonwealth quota for the crew had been 51 per cent.

The enumeration policy was designed to give the merchants of England the handling of those plantation products which were consigned to an ultimate foreign destination. Such products had to be landed in England and pass the customs. They might then, as a separate transaction, be re-exported as if they had been English goods. The object was mercantile profit rather than revenue, for a drawback of the whole or part of the duty paid on landing was usually allowed. So far, the stapling policy applied only to traffic inwards from the colonies. Its complement, the stapling of the outward traffic, was applied by the Staple Act of 1663, which prohibited the transport of goods from European countries directly to the colonies, even in English ships, and forced such goods to pass through England.

These two Acts, of 1660 and 1663, formed the core of the whole system known as the Laws of Trade and Navigation. Numerous later Acts were for the purpose of amending details and coping with the ceaseless efforts at evasion on the part of the colonists. For good and evil the system remained substantially in force until the third decade of the nineteenth century, when Huskisson procured the repeal of those parts of it that restricted the colonial trade.

The remainder of the system, reserving the coasting trade and requiring that English ships should be English-manned, was repealed by the free-traders of 1849, since which time it has been possible for a British ship to be built and owned abroad and to be manned entirely by foreigners, from captain to cabin-boy. The enthusiasts of 1849 paid no consideration to national defence, which they held to be a thing of the past, since wars were to be eliminated from a free-trading world.

For good and evil, then, the statesmen of the Restoration made permanent the system constructed by those of the Commonwealth. The evil has always been sufficiently apparent. From the outset the colonies complained. Sir William Berkeley, the Governor of

Virginia, protested against the Act of 1660 as soon as he heard of it, and Lord Willoughby, the Governor of the Caribbee Islands, wrote bitterly to Charles II that whoever had advised the King to restrict the colonial trade was more a merchant than a good subject. The sense of grievance never subsided, and not even the most loyal of colonists could conceive that he was doing anything morally wrong in evading these Acts passed by a Parliament in which he was not represented. Enforcement of the Acts was sometimes slack, sometimes fairly effective, but never complete; and when effective it was easy to describe it as tyranny. Evasion was always evident, and at times it predominated.[1] The West Indian planters, living in islands easily patrolled, could be made to conform; but in the American colonies the long coast-line presented great difficulties to the King's officers, and law-breaking became a habit which did not die out with Independence. The modern attitude of Americans towards restrictive laws, even of their own making, an attitude illustrated on the greatest scale in the resistance to Prohibition, is in part a legacy from the warfare of the past against the Laws of Trade and Navigation.

Much more than this can be said, and justly said, against the system. In its own good time a good deal was said on the British side in its favour. Almost every publicist and economist of the mother country, until the late eighteenth century, firmly believed that it was essential to wealth and defence. Without the Navigation Acts, they contended, there could be no Navy adequate for its duties; and the Navy protected the colonies from foreign conquest no less than the British Isles. That was undoubtedly true, although the colonists were slow to acknowledge it, for they seldom saw

[1] The effects of the Acts are clearly traced in Beer's later work, *The Old Colonial System*, 2 vols., New York, 1910.

the Navy in operation as anything but a police force chasing illicit traders: the great naval campaigns that defended the colonies were conducted for the most part in European waters, and there was little attempt to explain their significance across the Atlantic. Towards the end of the eighteenth century doubts were cast upon the commercial advantages of the system by Adam Smith and others. Smith's finding was that it impeded trade, but he admitted that it strengthened the country's sea power; and since, to quote his own words, 'defence is of much more importance than opulence', he concluded that the Navigation Act of 1660 was on the whole a wise measure.

The War of Independence shook what faith remained in the wisdom of the Laws of Trade and Navigation, and the commentators of the nineteenth century had in general nothing good to say for them. It was agreed that they had been wholly pernicious, not only to imperial harmony, but to the commercial objects primarily sought by their creators. The complete contradiction between the nineteenth-century and eighteenth-century views would appear to imply that one or the other was radically unsound. It has been the work of the less abstract and more historically minded economists of the past half-century to resolve the contradiction by drawing attention to the change of circumstances between one period and the other. The immense industrial energy of the nineteenth century rendered production the chief employment of England, and unimpeded disposal, without any restriction of its channels, imperative. But in the seventeenth and eighteenth centuries English production was not supreme over that of other countries, and its own strength was not sufficient to attract the flow of raw materials. Artificial canalization of the supply had therefore much to be said for it, while the more intimate connexion between the mercantile and fighting navies, and the warlike statesmanship of the times, rendered the deliberate fostering of shipping a necessity. It is probably true that the industrial supremacy of nineteenth-century England would never have come into being without the antecedent supremacy of the Navy that won Trafalgar, and recent historians concede with Adam Smith that that wonderful Navy was the child of the Navigation Acts.

The importance of the Newfoundland fishery in the national view of oceanic interests was so great as to be hard to realize in the changed conditions of the present day. A prolonged controversy raged round it in the Stuart period, and even later. Under the Tudors the fishery had been carried on exclusively by mariners from Europe, who went out in the spring and came home in the late summer; and there had been no colonial inhabitants on the scene of action. Under the early Stuarts several little English settlements took root in the Avalon Peninsula, which forms the south-east corner of the island. The settlers made their living in the fishery and traded with the merchants of New England. They were known as the boat-fishermen, in contrast with the ship-fishermen who came from the western ports of England. The ship-fishermen displayed the utmost animosity towards the colonial boat-fishermen, and agitated ceaselessly for the extinction of the colony. Mercantile and political opinion supported this contention. It was argued that the ship-fishery was a most gainful trade for England, since its produce was for the most part sold to the Mediterranean countries at good profit, while the outlay was solely upon ships and mariners whose existence was a national benefit. Then, again, the ship-fishermen were valuable above all others to the Navy, for they were regularly in their home ports in the winter. To mobilize the fleet it needed only to stop their spring sailing and draft them, to the number of from 5,000 to 10,000, into the King's ships. With the advisers of Charles II the arguments for the home monopoly very nearly carried the day. Orders were issued that no settlers in Newfoundland were to dwell within six miles of the coast, and, this not proving enforceable, it was decided in 1675 to deport all the inhabitants. The Newfoundland colony appeared to be doomed, but was saved at the last moment by the existence of a rival French settlement in the same quarter of the island. Sir John Berry, the naval officer sent out to remove the boat-fishermen, reported that it would be impossible to prevent them from taking refuge under the French flag. This gave pause to the home government, which reflected that the presence of a strong French colony and the absence of an English one would ultimately create a claim for a French monopoly of the fishery. The colony was accordingly reprieved, although the arguments against it continued to be revived far on into the eighteenth century.

The whole story is yet another illustration of the developed English view of Atlantic enterprise. By the late seventeenth century a colony was valuable only as it employed English shipping and yielded a favourable balance of trade. Newfoundland very nearly lost its existence by failing to satisfy the test. Sir Josiah Child, Governor of the East India Company and the author of the most closely reasoned mercantile treatise of the late seventeenth century,[1] thus generalized the doctrine: 'All colonies and foreign plantations do endamage their mother-kingdom, whereof the trades of such plantations are not confined to their said mother-kingdom by good laws and severe execution of those laws.'

[1] *A New Discourse of Trade*, London, 1694.

VI

THE OPENING OF THE PACIFIC

As soon as it was recognized that North America was a new continent not identical with Asia, it was evident that an unknown ocean must exist between them. The Spaniard Balboa first saw this ocean after marching across the Isthmus of Panama in 1513; and since he viewed it looking southwards from the Isthmus, he named it the South Sea. Seven years later, in 1520, Magellan first sailed a European ship across its whole extent from America to Asia, and he named it the Pacific Ocean. Both names have therefore the authority of pioneers fully entitled to bestow them. Magellan's has prevailed in modern times, but for a long period Balboa's was more commonly used, even in formal contexts, as when the British government chartered the South Sea Company in 1711. A variant of it, with a somewhat different and not closely defined meaning, is still employed by seamen, who speak of the great stretch of open water round the world, roughly south of the latitudes of the Cape of Good Hope and Australia, as the Southern Ocean.

From the time of its discovery until nearly the end of the eighteenth century, the problems presented by the Pacific to European enterprise fall into two main categories: first, the utilization of the ocean as a means of access to eastern Asia; and second, the discovery of the lands expected to exist in its vast expanse, and especially of the great southern continent, Terra Australis Incognita, almost universally believed to lie in its southern temperate and tropical latitudes and to extend right round the world. The progress of this enterprise may be studied in three periods, very roughly approximating to three successive centuries. The sixteenth century was the period of Spanish and some English exploration; the seventeenth was that mainly of Dutch effort; and the eighteenth was that of the British preponderantly, with the French as a good second. We shall here be concerned chiefly with the work of our own countrymen, although, in order to make it clear, the achievements of others must be kept in sight.

Access to Asia had been the motive of the pioneer Atlantic voyages which had revealed America. The discovery of the great continental barrier did not put an end to the western quest for Asia, but altered its method. The object became to find a passage round either end of the Americas or through them. The northern voyages all failed to yield a passage. The central ones, in tropical latitudes, also found no sea-channel, but did show that America narrowed to an isthmus, which Balboa first crossed. The southern dis covery, under Magellan, was successful, and his Straits provided a way by which ships could sail westward from Europe to the Far East. Magellan discovered the Philippine Islands and was killed there, but one of his vessels came home to Spain by circumnavigating the globe in a continuous westerly direction. Another tried to return across the Pacific to America, but was foiled by the winds, put back to the Moluccas, and was there taken by the Portuguese.

The Spanish thirst for conquest was by no means satiated by Mexico and Peru, and Spaniards at once took up the ambitions of trading with the Far East and discovering new lands in the Pacific. For some forty years they were defeated by the difficulties of Pacific navigation. With great risk and hardship they sailed through the Straits of Magellan and reached the Asiatic islands, but they could not achieve the return voyage, owing to the prevalent easterly winds of the tropic zone both north and south of the equator. To carry on the Eastern trade by circumnavigation, as Magellan's survivors had done, was not part of their plan, for Spain admitted the Portuguese monopoly of the Indian Ocean and the Cape of Good Hope. Several Spanish expeditions came to grief by failing to recross the Pacific, and it was not until 1565 that the problem was solved. In that year a Spanish commander, who had been to the Philippines with a colonizing party, found the way back by casting north-wards into the belt of westerly winds, which brought him across to the coast of California, whence he made his way south to Mexico. A small but regular Spanish trade was thenceforth established. Manila in the Philippines became an entrepôt for traffic with China. Mexican silver there purchased Chinese silks, porce-lain, and other rich goods, and also, for some time, gold at an extremely favourable valuation in relation to silver. The sailing of one, two, or more richly laden vessels, known as the Manila galleons, became an annual event, and the goods were forwarded through Mexico by the plate fleets to Europe. Spaniards had long since given up using the dangerous Straits of Magellan, finding it much easier to tranship Pacific goods through Mexico or Panama.

The ability to recross the Pacific revived Spanish ambitions to discover the unknown continent of Terra Australis, which all geographers declared to exist as the southern border of the great ocean. Since the investigation of this mainly non-existent continent became a major incentive to the explorers of four maritime nations until the latter part of the eighteenth century, the origins of the belief in it must be briefly described. The classical geographers, having proved that the earth was a sphere and that great land-masses

occupied its northern hemisphere, had argued that
there must be comparable land-masses in the southern
hemisphere to balance the weight of the northern
masses. Land was heavier than water, and the sphere,
they conceived, floated motionless in space with its
northern surface uppermost. It could not do so unless
there was something more massive than unbroken sea
in the southern hemisphere. The idea persisted through
the Middle Ages and was unquestioned by the Renaissance. When Magellan passed through his Strait, with
land of unknown extent to the southward, this Tierra
del Fuego was accepted as part of the great southern
continent. Some ten years later a number of map-
makers began to depict a land-mass far away to the
westward, where the South Sea verged on the Indian
Ocean. They named it Java the Great and placed it
approximately where Australia actually exists. It may
represent a Portuguese discovery of Australia, otherwise unrecorded.[1] The next step was taken by academic geographers, who linked Terra del Fuego with
Java the Great to make a complete continental border,
fringing the whole of the South Pacific in latitudes
from 50° to 30°. This conception took firm shape in
the 1560's, and its gradual demolition occupied the
following two hundred years. Not content with a continent in the South Pacific, the geographers extended
it both ways to close in the South Atlantic and the
Indian Ocean, and made of it a roughly circular land-
cap covering all the southern regions of the globe, in
area the greatest of all the continents. But the Pacific
part of it was always the focus of interest, for it was
held to project farthest into temperate climates. In

[1] This is one of the unsettled questions in the history of discovery. The
late G. A. Wood, in *The Discovery of Australia*, London, 1922, held that it
was settled in the adverse sense—that there was no discovery; but his
handling of the evidence is open to serious criticism, and the subject still
awaits full investigation.

the Pacific section were located King Solomon's Land of Ophir and the rich kingdoms of Locach and Malaiur recorded by Marco Polo.[1]

In search of these lands Alvaro de Mendaña sailed from Peru in 1567. He discovered a group of large islands a few degrees south of the equator, and named them the Islands of King Solomon. He believed that they contained gold and that the main continent lay not far to the south-west. On this assumption the discovery resembled that of the Antilles by Columbus, with the promise of similar rich conquests to follow. Mendaña returned by the North Pacific to Mexico, and thence to Peru. Personal jealousies prevented him from following up the work for many years, and meanwhile the English entered the South Sea. Englishmen in Mexico reported the discovery of the Solomon Islands, and in the early 'seventies there was formed the project of Sir Richard Grenville and his friends for the exploitation of Terra Australis. We have considered that project in dealing with the Tudor propagandists, and since Grenville was not able to act upon it, we need not speak further of it here.

The first Englishmen actually to sail on the Pacific were John Oxenham and his crew, who crossed the Isthmus and captured Spanish vessels carrying treasure from Peru to Panama. Much new information about Oxenham has recently come to light in documents discovered at Seville and published by the Hakluyt Society.[2] They show that, had he succeeded, he intended to occupy the Isthmus permanently and cut the treasure-route from Peru to Spain. They also correct the date previously assigned to his adventure: it

[1] The Atlas of Abraham Ortelius, published in 1570, clearly shows this conception of Terra Australis. He says that some were then calling it the Magellanic continent.

[2] I. A. Wright, *Documents concerning the English Voyages to the Spanish Main, 1569–80*, Hakluyt Society, 1932.

was not 1575, but 1576–7. Oxenham, however, after causing immense anxiety to the Spaniards, was captured and hanged by them.

Next came Drake, who sailed in 1577 on a voyage intended by his backers to achieve great new discoveries and empire-building. Recent research has found important new evidence on Drake's voyage;[1] and, even though many of its problems are not cleared up, the outline of the story has been revolutionized. Drake, it now appears, was sent out to pass the Straits of Magellan and investigate the coast of Terra Australis Incognita, where, it was expected, would be found civilized inhabitants and markets for English goods. In effect, he was to carry out the project put forward by Grenville four years earlier. The Queen had revoked her consent to Grenville's venture, because she feared that he would attack the Spaniards instead of prosecuting discoveries.[2] She now not only licensed Drake to make the voyage, but herself instigated him to convert it into a treasure raid, official Anglo-Spanish relations having changed for the worse in the interim. Drake therefore, after leaving the Straits, turned northwards for Chile and Peru instead of north-westwards for Terra Australis. It is possible that he meant to co-operate with Oxenham on the Isthmus and perhaps join forces with him for the capture of Panama; for when Drake had sailed, the defeat of Oxenham had been unknown in England. If such was the plan, Drake soon learned that it was impossible, for the first Spanish prisoners whom he questioned were able to tell him that Oxenham was in captivity at Lima.

[1] E. G. R. Taylor, 'The Missing Draft Project of Drake's Voyage', *Geographical Journal*, January, 1930; and 'More Light on Drake', *Mariner's Mirror*, April, 1930.
[2] These facts about Grenville were revealed by Oxenham and John Butler when under examination by their Spanish captors. See Z. Nuttall, *New Light on Drake*, Hakluyt Society, 1914, pp. 6–7, 11.

This connexion between Drake and Oxenham is quite conjectural, but it is a tenable conjecture opened up by the establishment of the true date of Oxenham's voyage. The two men were old comrades, and Oxenham admitted to the Spaniards that he had discussed his plans with Drake, and further, that he knew Drake's intention of entering the South Sea by the Straits. If Oxenham's expedition had succeeded in mastering the Isthmus, as the Spaniards at one time feared it would, and Drake had then appeared on the Pacific side with armed shipping, there would have been the brilliant possibility, not only of cutting off the Peruvian treasure from Spain, but ultimately of diverting it to England. Spain at that time had comparatively few men on the west coast of America, and not a single armed ship, and in fact, scarcely any heavy guns on land. Such may have been the plan at which Elizabeth connived when she gave secret leave to Drake to work his will with the expedition.

As it was, Drake, who had parted company with two of his ships in tempestuous weather to the southward, had to do his best with the *Golden Hind* alone, and without any co-operation from the land. He raided various seaports up the coast, and secured the bulk of his booty by the capture of the unarmed treasure-ship *Cacafuego*. The Spaniards believed that he meant to proceed to Panama, the safety of that city being their chief preoccupation, but he did not do so. Instead, he passed to seaward and went on up the west coast of Mexico. Far in the south, round about the exit of the Straits of Magellan, he had been driven to and fro by two months of heavy gales, and had made the discovery that there was in that region no sign of a southern continent, but that Tierra del Fuego was only an island of moderate size. Now once more, after he quitted the Mexican coast, the voyage became one of discovery. It has been said that he feared to seek his homeward passage by the Straits because he guessed that a Spanish force would lie in wait there. The Spaniards indeed had a number of ships, but since not one of them was armed, the reasoning is not very probable. It is more likely that Drake deliberately preferred to resume the original plan of the voyage. Terra Australis, if it anywhere existed, was now too far away, but the Grenville proposals had included also the opening of trade with Asia, and the discovery of the North West Passage from the Pacific side; and to these objects Drake proceeded. The Pacific offered more than one field for English expansion.

Contemporary geographers placed the Pacific opening of the North West Passage in the latitude of about 40 degrees. Drake went considerably higher than this latitude and then sailed back along the coast without finding any channel. He stayed a month to refit at a Californian anchorage which has never been satisfactorily identified, but which was not far from the modern San Francisco. He made friends with the natives and annexed the country in the Queen's name, setting up a metal plate with a record of the circumstances. In 1936 a roughly inscribed brass plate was picked up near San Francisco, and is now the property of the University of California. Although some have suspected it to be a fake, and have advanced serious grounds for scepticism, the evidence in its favour is also impressive, and on present information it seems reasonable to accept the plate as that veritably set up by Francis Drake in 1579.[1] Since it was not found as Drake placed it but had evidently been moved, the identification of his anchorage is not greatly assisted by the discovery.

Drake regarded further search for a passage to the

[1] The circumstances of the discovery of the plate are briefly recorded by the present writer in *Geographical Journal*, June 1938.

Atlantic as unprofitable, and set sail across the Pacific in the zone of the north-east trades. In so doing he was making discoveries that were new only to Englishmen, for Spaniards had long been making the voyage. He reached the Moluccas, laded some tons of spices at Ternate, and came home by the Indian Ocean and the Cape. His expedition was the first English circumnavigation, and the first English crossing of the Pacific and the Indian Oceans, appropriately emphasized by the acquisition of Western treasure and Eastern spices. Drake's own account of the voyage, known to have been presented to the Queen, has never been seen by any historian, and must now be regarded as lost. Published accounts by men who sailed with him are superficial, in important passages meagre, and even deliberately obscure.

Drake's voyage had important negative results on Pacific exploration. To Spain it acted as a direct deterrent, for the Spanish statesmen concluded that to make fresh discoveries would simply provide fresh attractions and facilities for the English enemy. All surplus energies in Chile and Peru were therefore directed to defence, and Mendaña's hopes of proceeding to Australian discovery were blighted. Not until 1595, when the defences of the west coast had proved themselves adequate, was he allowed to try again. He was old and worn out, and died on the voyage, in which he failed to reach the Solomon Islands although he did discover the Marquesas and Santa Cruz. Drake's two successes, in treasure-raiding and spice-trading, deterred the English also from further attempts upon Terra Australis; for the demonstrated profits outweighed the hypothetical. Thomas Cavendish went through the Straits in 1586 and turned northward for Peru. He found that the Spaniards were arming themselves, and 'made' his voyage only by the capture of a galleon returning to Mexico from Manila. He also crossed the Pacific and circumnavigated the world. Other expeditions, including a second led by Cavendish, failed to get through the Straits. The last of the series, under Richard Hawkins in 1593–4, did so, but only to be brought to action and captured by the heavily armed squadron which Spain had now stationed on the Peruvian coast. After Hawkins's disaster no other English ship is known to have entered the Pacific for nearly eighty years.

It was some years after Drake's voyage before all geographers agreed in pushing back the southern continent to the southward of Tierra del Fuego, although the best-informed Englishmen knew from his experience that there was an open sea passage as an alternative to using the Straits. Richard Hawkins, writing in 1602, plainly stated the fact. The first ships which actually passed into the Pacific through open water were those commanded by the Dutchmen Schouten and Le Maire in 1616. These commanders sighted and named Cape Horn. But the Southern Continent was thought to be near. Hawkins in 1594 had sailed along the northern side of the Falkland Islands, and assumed that they were part of the continent. Schouten and Le Maire likewise assumed that their discovery of Staten Island was a projection of the great land-mass. On the Pacific side the conception of a long coastline running diagonally north-westwards remained unchanged. English interest in the region still continued in the reign of James I. Sir Richard Hawkins was twice in negotiation with the East India Company for the command of an expedition to rediscover the Solomon Islands, and thence presumably to proceed to Terra Australis.[1] Sir William Courteen petitioned the Crown for a grant

[1] *The Observations of Sir Richard Hawkins*, ed. J. A. Williamson, London, 1933, Introd., pp. lxxxvi–lxxxvii.

of trading and colonizing rights in all the unknown lands of the South, whether in the Atlantic or the Pacific. But nothing came of these projects, for the North Atlantic and East Indian expansions were absorbing all the energies of the English people.

With the exception of one important Spanish voyage, the early seventeenth century was the period of Dutch discovery in the South Sea. The Spanish expedition of two ships sailed from Peru in 1606 under the command of Fernandez de Quiros. His aim was to complete the work of Mendaña by discovering the tropical part of Terra Australis Incognita which was assumed to lie where the true Australia actually does lie. He did not go quite far enough, but reached the largest island of the New Hebrides, which he thought to be continental and named Austrialia del Espiritu Santo. The insubordination of his crew compelled Quiros at this point to turn back and part company with his second ship. That vessel, under two officers named Torres and Prado, pushed on to an important discovery. They passed along the unknown south side of New Guinea and threaded the dangerous strait that separates it from Australia. By so doing they proved the insularity of New Guinea, which had hitherto been uncertain, some geographers having declared it to be part of the great southern continent. Their discovery, however, did not pass into public knowledge. Both officers wrote accounts of the voyage, but the Spanish government, either by neglect or intention, omitted to publish them. The manuscript of Torres came to light in the mid-eighteenth century, when justice was at length done by the naming of his discovery Torres Strait. Prado's account was found only in our own time, and was first published in 1930.[1]

[1] In *New Light on the Discovery of Australia*, ed. H. N. Stevens, Hakluyt Society, 1930.

The Dutch involuntarily discovered Western Australia in the course of their voyages from the Cape of Good Hope to the spice archipelago, but this coast was in the Indian Ocean and not in the Pacific. Their deliberate explorations all proceeded from their Eastern head-quarters in Java. In 1606 and the following years they investigated parts of Northern Australia and gradually realized that it was a land continuous with the Western discoveries. They did not know that Torres had found the strait between Australia and New Guinea, and did not discover it themselves. On the contrary, they believed that the two lands were joined, an error that persisted until Captain Cook's time. The most important South Sea exploration by the Dutch was accomplished in one great voyage under the command of Abel Tasman. Its inspiration was strategic. In the 1640's the Dutch were at war with Spain and had visions of attacking Peru from the East Indies. The only known means of doing so was by the great circuit through the North Pacific to California and thence by coasting southwards. In the tropic zones, north and south of the equator, the trade-winds were from the east and contrary. Anthony van Diemen, the Governor-General of the Dutch Indies, wished to learn whether South America could be approached by utilizing the belt of westerly winds to the south of the tropics. If the seas were open in those latitudes, it would be possible; if the unknown continent projected too far northwards, the voyagers would be deflected into the trade-wind belt and their progress stopped. In 1642 Van Diemen sent Tasman to investigate.

Tasman sailed from Batavia into the Indian Ocean and pressed south into the latitudes of the strong westerly gales. These carried him well to the south of the Australian coast, and out of sight of it until he came to the land now called Tasmania. He named it

Van Diemen's Land after his patron, and rounded it by the south. Thence he pushed on westwards on the track to South America until he met with another obstacle. He called it New Zealand and assumed it to be part of Terra Australis Incognita. It is noteworthy how this purely academic conception misled explorer after explorer and caused them to adopt wrong interpretations which would never have occurred to them if only they had been ignorant of geographical science. New Zealand was the fifth southern island to be hailed as the missing continent,[1] and there were more to follow. Being quite sure that he was on the coast of Terra Australis, Tasman followed it northwards, and was pleased to find that it came to an end (at Cape Maria van Diemen) in a latitude where west winds could still be counted on. Here he concluded that his mission was accomplished and that he had demonstrated the feasibility of the new track to South America, for, with the academic maps still in his mind, he conceived the continent as trending away southeastwards to Schouten's discovery in the neighbourhood of Cape Horn. This time his conclusion was right, although his premisses were false. It was not his task to go on to America in person. He therefore took a wide circle through the tropics, passed through the Fiji group (a new discovery), and returned to Batavia by the north side of New Guinea.

Tasman had contributed more to knowledge than any previous explorer since Magellan. In addition to what has been described, he had proved that the true Australia must have an eastern coast, although he had not seen that coast, having passed hundreds of miles clear of it. But Tasman had circumnavigated the true Australia, and by so doing had carved another large

[1] The previous four were Tierra del Fuego, the Falklands, Espiritu Santo, and Staten Island.

slice off the diminishing Terra Australis Incognita, although he had unnecessarily added a slice to it in the shape of New Zealand.

Tasman made another voyage on the northern coast of Australia, but the grand South Pacific investigations of both himself and his countrymen began and ended with the voyage of 1642–3. Two years later Van Diemen died, and his scheme of attacking Peru was abandoned. In the North Pacific the Dutch made some progress with charting the coasts of Japan. They heard and believed stories of a great civilized land with white inhabitants between Japan and North America, but their efforts to find it resulted only in the sighting of the Kurile Islands. For nearly sixty years after Tasman's time the history of South Sea exploration is a blank.

Towards the end of the seventeenth century the English reappeared in the Pacific. There was indeed one earlier incursion, but it was entirely without significance. In 1669 Charles II sent a naval captain, Sir John Narborough, through the Straits of Magellan, presumably to reconnoitre the prospects. Narborough reached Valparaiso, was badly treated by the authorities there, and returned by the way he had come, having accomplished nothing. In 1681 a more important movement took place. Some parties of buccaneers, for the most part English, crossed the Isthmus from the Caribbean, and captured Spanish shipping in the South Sea. After seeking plunder without great success on the Peruvian coast they recrossed the Isthmus and dispersed in the West Indies. Again in 1683–4 a buccaneer expedition sailed from Virginia southwards to Cape Horn and so into the Pacific. This party also had little success and broke up. One of its ships crossed the great ocean to the Philippines, and thence wandered through the Eastern Archipelago until in

1688 it sighted the north-western coast of Australia. Its further adventures were in the Indian Ocean and do not concern us here. Indeed, the whole of the proceedings of these buccaneers would be irrelevant to our purpose but for the fact that in both of the expeditions there sailed one remarkable individual, William Dampier.

Dampier was by profession a seaman, he rose to be a captain, and he was given the charge of an exploring expedition by the British government. But he was not a great seaman, commander, or explorer; in fact, in the last two capacities he was substantially a failure. Yet he was demonstrably the originator of the modern British interest in the Pacific and the inspirer of the successful efforts of the eighteenth century to clear up the mysteries of the ocean. He achieved those effects by his writings, which were widely read at the time of their publication and continued to influence the national thought throughout the eighteenth century.

The buccaneers of Dampier's time were in their declining stage. Their leaders were less able than those of the earlier generation, and they themselves were not distinguishable from common pirates, save in the fact that they did not commit wanton atrocities on their prisoners. But they did rob indiscriminately any shipping that fell into their power, and their way of life was criminal. Dampier joined these men willingly and did not find their proceedings obnoxious to his conscience. He did, however, find their society increasingly uncongenial, as they did his, for the qualities of his mind and the range of his interests rendered him suspect to the drunken illiterates who composed the buccaneer crew. After leaving the Australian coast he managed to part company with his comrades and came home to England in a merchantman by way of the Cape of Good Hope. Altogether he had taken twelve years to drift round the world, without rising to leadership and without acquiring any wealth in the process.

In 1697 Dampier published his first book, *A New Voyage round the World*.[1] Its success was immediate, and he became known as an authority on the Isthmus of Panama, the Pacific, and the East Indies. In the capacity of an expert witness he gave evidence on various occasions before the Council of Trade and Plantations. His book revived an interest in the South Sea that had been almost dead since Drake's time; and the impending problem of the Spanish Succession, involving the disposal of Peru and Panama and other rich territories, urged statesmen to take account of the possibilities. For these reasons the Admiralty decided to send out an exploring expedition to investigate the unknown parts of Terra Australis, and to appoint Dampier to the command. They allotted him a decayed vessel named the *Roebuck* with a crew of impressed nondescripts, for the most part unfit and unwilling, and they delayed the preparations until the best season of the year for the purpose in mind had been lost. Dampier's purpose was to explore the unknown eastern face of Australia. He wished to approach it from the eastward by rounding Cape Horn, but the loss of the summer season caused him to sail by the Cape of Good Hope. He thus came to Western Australia, already known and regarded as valueless. Thence he proceeded to Timor and the adjacent islands, little known to the English, and passed along the northern side of New Guinea, then universally believed to be part of Australia. Having arrived at the eastern end of New Guinea, Dampier knew that to the southward there stretched the hundreds of miles of unknown coast which he had come to discover. But

[1] Modern edition by Sir Albert Gray, London, 1927.

at this point he turned back, for reasons of unfitness of ship and crew which appear to be adequate enough. His only discovery had been that of the separation of New Britain from New Guinea by the strait now called Dampier Passage. On the homeward voyage the *Roebuck* sank in calm weather from perfect age and rottenness. All hands were saved, and Dampier was acquitted of blame. But by another court-martial he was condemned to lose all his pay for harsh treatment of one of his officers, who seems to have deserved it, and was declared unfit to command any of the Queen's ships thereafter.

This was the sum of Dampier's work as a discoverer. He may be classified as the first of a series of eighteenth-century explorers who drew near to the eastern side of Australia, but failed to close with it. His true importance lay in his writings. The *New Voyage* ran into several editions. A continuation called *Voyages and Discoveries* came out in 1699,[1] while the *Voyage to New Holland* was described in two volumes published in 1703 and 1709 respectively,[2] after which Dampier wrote nothing of moment. His writing career therefore occupied twelve years and produced three books. They were mainly on a new subject, the South Sea, and they treated it in a new style, that of popularized science. Dampier was well equipped for interesting a wide public in the science of Nature displayed, for he had a scientific mind untrammelled by a scientific education. He was a painstaking observer and an assiduous recorder, a clear and logical thinker with the courage of his convictions and the candour to admit his mistakes; and he viewed phenomena with the eye of an intelligent, unlearned man, and described them for such men in unacademic language of admirable vigour

[1] Modern edition by Clennell Wilkinson, London, 1931.
[2] Modern edition by the present writer, London, 1939.

and clarity. The consequence was that all sorts of people read him for pleasure and for profit. For the naturalist he described birds, beasts, fish, and flowers. For the navigator he was full of professional detail on soundings, winds, and compass variation. For the merchant he noted commodities, and for the statesman strategic possibilities. And for all England there set in a new sensation that was to grow strong as the eighteenth century advanced, the romance of unknown lands and peoples, and especially those of the South Sea.

For half a century the effects, so far as England was concerned, remained speculative and literary, until, with the reign of George III, a new period of intensive exploration began, which in the space of fifteen years solved all the major problems of the South Sea.

The speculative period is full of interest, for it illustrates those problems and the theories arising from them. The Spanish Succession War was naturally not conducive to exploration, although it did give occasion for a number of privateering expeditions into the well-known parts of the Pacific. One of these, led by Dampier, was a complete failure. He had no talent for war or command, and was invariably on bad terms with his subordinates. Another, under Captain Woodes Rogers of Bristol, was a brilliant success, and here Dampier served as navigating officer, a position which gave employment for his real ability, which was scientific. Woodes Rogers captured much booty in the tropical Pacific and circumnavigated the globe in the manner of Drake. His account of the achievement, published under the title *A Cruising Voyage round the World*,[1] has been reprinted in recent years and is well worth reading. These voyages added nothing to geographical knowledge, although they stimulated commercial interest.

[1] London, 1712.

One result was the foundation in 1711 of the South Sea Company, whose operations are for us irrelevant, since it never sent a ship into the South Sea.

The return of peace gave leisure for reflection and projection. An abortive project of 1715 has recently come to light, and illustrates the trend of thought. One John Welbe, who had sailed with Dampier, requested the government of George I to give him the command of two ships, with which he proposed to sail round Cape Horn and cross the Pacific to explore the unknown Eastern Australia, taking up the work at the point where Dampier had laid it down. Welbe's record was not one to inspire confidence. The highest rank he had attained at sea was that of midshipman, and he remarked in his proposition that he possessed not two shillings in the world. The ministry of 1715 took no action, perhaps considering that a person who had reached middle age without accumulating two shillings had not given evidence of the prudence requisite for an important command.[1] In fact, from this time onwards the Admiralty, taught by its somewhat unhappy experience with Dampier, never entrusted the leadership of exploring expeditions to any but regular naval officers of proved character and talent.

On the purely literary side the *Travels of Lemuel Gulliver* illustrate the extent of the unknown regions of the Pacific and the romantic possibilities contained in them. Swift had no interest in commerce or practical exploration, but he had to locate his fantastic lands in plausible positions. Two centuries earlier Sir Thomas More had placed his Utopia in unknown South America. Swift was obliged to range wider. His Lilliput

[1] Welbe's scheme, with an accompanying letter, occurs in a MS. volume of Naval Miscellanea in the Library of the National Maritime Museum. The document is printed in the present writer's Introduction to the *Voyage to New Holland*, pp. lx–lxii.

was in south-eastern Australia, Brobdingnag in the North Pacific, east of Japan, Balnibarbi farther over towards northern California, while the land of the Houyhnhnms was placed in that part of the unknown southern continent which fronted the Indian Ocean. The privateering voyages had drawn attention to the importance of Juan Fernandez as a place of assembly and refit for operations against the Spanish treasure coast, and one of them had occasioned the residence of Alexander Selkirk on the island. But the contribution of Selkirk to Defoe's *Robinson Crusoe* has been greatly exaggerated. Crusoe's island bore no resemblance to Juan Fernandez and was set in a different ocean, and the book could have been written equally well if Selkirk had never existed. All its geographical circumstances are drawn from quite other sources of information than Selkirk's adventure.

In one respect the South Sea interest of the eighteenth century resembled the Atlantic interest of Elizabeth's time: it inspired the publication of collections of voyages and discoveries, with whose narratives there was sometimes mingled propaganda. Since the days of Hakluyt and Purchas there had been no new English collection of sea adventures, but under Queen Anne the publishers began to turn again to this kind of work, and the existence of a public for it was undoubtedly due to the stimulus of Dampier. In 1704 a London publisher[1] brought out *A Collection of Voyages and Travels*, and next year a rival[2] produced *A Compleat Collection* of the same. Dampier's books were frequently reprinted, until in 1729 they became a collection of South Sea voyages, the so-called four-volume Dampier, which includes a good deal of matter written by other hands.

[1] John Churchill, 4 volumes in 1704, but vols. v and vi added in 1732.
[2] John Harris, 2 vols.

Particularly interesting is John Campbell's *Collection* of 1744–8, an augmentation of that of 1705, for Campbell put forward a comprehensive plan for the exploitation of the South Sea. He was much impressed with Dampier's description of New Britain, the island discovered and named by that navigator at the eastern end of New Guinea. New Britain, said Campbell, had the makings of a head-quarters for valuable tropical trade. To the north of it were the known amenities of the Asiatic Indies, not all occupied by the Dutch. To the south lay the unexplored possibilities of Eastern Australia. The difficulty was in the vast distance from Europe. To meet that difficulty Campbell proposed the occupation and fortification of Juan Fernandez off the coast of Chile, an island unused by the Spaniards, although visited by their enemies for the purpose of watering and refitting. The permanent retention of Juan Fernandez, he estimated, would need a garrison of five hundred men. It would serve as a refreshing-place for ships from England after they had rounded Cape Horn, and it was within a two months' voyage of Australia with the south-east trades. Campbell urged yet another advantage from his plan. The primary discovery to be made would be that of Eastern Australia, but there was also the prospect of finding Terra Australis Incognita between the known Australia and South America. Belief in its existence had been stimulated by the report of a buccaneer captain named Davis, who asserted that he had sighted a continent in 27° S. and about 1,500 miles west of Chile. Davis Land, which may have been Easter Island or may have been wholly imaginary, was important in the South Sea plans of the early eighteenth century.

Shortly before Campbell advocated the colonization of Juan Fernandez, Commodore George Anson had visited the island in the course of his famous circumnavigation, the best-remembered episode of the Jenkins' Ear War. Anson had been sent out to attack the Spaniards on the west coast of South America, but his ill-found expedition had suffered so badly from the gales of Cape Horn that he was able to make only a superficial raid. The true intention of the British government had undoubtedly been more serious, for Anson's instructions had contemplated the possibility of detaching the South American colonies from Spain and setting them up as independent States. These would naturally be open to the trade of Great Britain and would afford a fine opportunity for exploiting the Pacific.[1] It is true to say that these South American ambitions were present in the minds of British statesmen right down to the dissolution of the Spanish Empire in the early nineteenth century, eighty years forward from Anson's expedition. In the other direction they link backwards to Cromwell and Drake. Campbell, in advocating the strategic value of Juan Fernandez, may very well have been aware of schemes that were not publicly disclosed.

The French, as Great Britain's rivals for colonial power, were also interested in the South, and in the interval between the Austrian Succession and Seven Years Wars a Frenchman produced an able and influential book on the subject, the *Histoire des Navigations aux Terres Australes*, by Charles de Brosses. This work combined the physical arguments for the existence of the southern continent with the historical records purporting to prove the discovery of various parts of it, and dilated in charming and persuasive style on the benefits to commerce, science, and civilization which would ensue from its complete exploration. De Brosses was a liberal-minded man of all-round benevolence,

---

[1] R. Pares, *War and Trade in the West Indies, 1739-63*, Oxford, 1936, pp. 65-77; the relevant passage in Anson's instructions is quoted on p. 76.

ardently patriotic, but desirous of weaning his country from the warlike ambitions of continental Europe. He had no doubt that the colonization of Terra Australis would be good for its inhabitants and for Frenchmen, including the criminals whom he wished to send out to be purified in the clean and innocent South.

The Seven Years War was the brutal answer of statesmanship to de Brosses's aspirations. It left the British with an easy confidence in their natural supremacy on the oceans, and the French with a hope that all was not lost and a determination to try again. Thus for both nations there was an incentive to transform speculation into practical effort in the Pacific.

The French were first at work, at least on the threshold of the Pacific. In the year of the Treaty of Paris an expedition sailed from St. Malo under Louis Antoine de Bougainville, a diplomatist and soldier who had turned navigator and was now to prove himself second only to Cook as an oceanic explorer. His mission was to take possession of the Falkland Islands, of which strategists were beginning to think highly as a base for South Sea enterprise. Early in 1764 Bougainville reached the islands, planted a little settlement in Berkeley Sound, and returned to France. Next year he went out again with supplies, and the colony promised well. Meanwhile the British Admiralty, having an inkling of these southern operations, but not knowing that a colony had been founded, sent out an expedition under Commodore John Byron, who had sailed under Anson twenty years before. Byron reached the Falklands in 1765, made a partial exploration without encountering the French, and, supposing the group to be uninhabited, took possession in the name of George III. He then passed on through the Straits of Magellan. He had been ordered to sail northwards to California, revive the claim to Drake's New Albion, and search the coast for a passage back to Hudson Bay and the Atlantic. But his crews were sickly, and he did none of these things. Instead, he crossed the Pacific with the trade-winds, and returned round the world by way of the Dutch Indies and the Cape of Good Hope. Since he crossed the Pacific by a well-known track he made no discoveries of any significance.[1]

Both the French and British enshrouded their plans for the Falkland Islands in complete secrecy. There ensued a comedy of errors that nearly resulted in a first-class war. Byron came home in 1766, and his report caused the British government to send out a frigate with a small colony in the same year. It was planted at Port Egmont, remote from the French, and nearly a year elapsed before either nationality became aware of the other's presence. A Spanish claim further complicated the situation. Spain protested to France that the islands were hers. France, having revised earlier impressions about the utility of the station, politely yielded to her ally, and Bougainville was sent out to hand over to Spanish officers from Buenos Ayres. The Spaniards then tackled the British, and in 1770 captured Port Egmont and forcibly removed its inhabitants. The British government demanded restitution under threat of war, and for a time it looked as though the two Bourbon Powers would fight. Ultimately they decided to give way, Port Egmont was restored, and the crisis passed; after which neither the British nor anyone else found any use for the Falklands, whose permanent colonization did not begin until the nineteenth century.

The exaggerated importance attached to these wind-swept islands had been based on their supposed indis-

[1] Byron's and the following voyages are recorded in J. C. Beaglehole's *Exploration of the Pacific*, London, 1934. Wherever possible Dr. Beaglehole gives the commanders' instructions.

pensability to Pacific enterprise, and the serious risk of a perfectly unnecessary war is a good example of statesmanship bemused by strategy. Meanwhile Pacific enterprise went on.

Three months after the return of Byron in 1766 the Admiralty dispatched two other captains, Samuel Wallis and Philip Carteret, to pass the Straits of Magellan and search for the unknown continent in the South Pacific. They took with them a store-ship with supplies for the colony in the Falklands, but did not themselves call there. After a long struggle with adverse winds they debouched from the Straits in April, 1767, and at once parted company in foul weather. They never rejoined, and from that point the enterprise splits into two distinct voyages.

Wallis in the *Dolphin* steered north-west and saw no continent. He did, however, discover several small units of the Tuamotus and in June sighted Tahiti, the most important island in this part of the South Sea. He named it King George the Third's Island and stayed five weeks to restore the health of his crew, who were suffering from scurvy. The men thoroughly enjoyed the completely comprehensive hospitality of the friendly natives, and discipline began to suffer. The ship, in fact, was in danger of being pulled to pieces when it was discovered that iron and copper nails were an acceptable currency for purchasing favours ashore; and Wallis, who was but a mild disciplinarian by the standards of his age, was glad to put to sea once more. He had discovered a large and populous island, but it offered no immediate commercial advantages. The remainder of his voyage was a comparatively uninteresting circumnavigation by way of the Philippines, the Dutch Indies, and the Cape of Good Hope. By steering north-west across the equator after leaving Tahiti, Wallis avoided closing with eastern Australia, where the greatest work was yet to be done.

The real hero of the expedition was Captain Philip Carteret. His little ship, the *Swallow*, was worn out and a poor sailer, lacking in necessary equipment, and apparently sent merely as a tender to the *Dolphin*. Nevertheless Carteret, when left to himself, made a more enterprising voyage than did Wallis. The true test of determination in these Pacific crossings was keeping a southerly course, for in the south, if anywhere, must lie the continent. But the farther south, the worse was the weather, and sooner or later scurvy and decay of gear compelled resort to the tropics for relief. Carteret followed a more southerly track than Wallis. By so doing he missed Tahiti, but established the non-existence of continental land in a hitherto untraversed belt. He then pressed on, with his men scurvy-stricken and his ship in a dangerous condition, refrained from turning northwards as Wallis had done, and rediscovered the Solomon Islands, exactly two hundred years after Mendaña had found them, two hundred years in which no other European had been there, and in which men had begun to say that the islands did not exist.[1] More than this, he continued to Dampier's New Britain, unvisited for sixty-seven years, and found that a strait cut it into two islands, of which he named the smaller New Ireland; and thence, with the ship ready to sink under him, by Northern New Guinea and the Moluccas to Batavia. He also had not pushed south-west to Australia, but who can blame him? The shipwrights at Batavia declared that the *Swallow* would never reach England, but under Carteret's command she did, having made the most plucky circumnavigation of the century.

[1] It is to be noted that Carteret did not recognize the identity of his islands with Mendaña's Solomons.

We left Bougainville handing over the French colony
in the Falklands to Spain. After doing so he passed the
Straits of Magellan early in 1768, and sailed into the
South Sea. Bougainville's orders were similar to those
of Wallis and Carteret, and his expedition led to similar
results. Like his predecessors, he sailed over what
should have been Davis Land and was satisfied that
no continent existed near the given position. Then he
came to Tahiti, some months after Wallis had left.
His report of the kindly natives and their pleasant,
carefree way of life did much to strengthen the cult of
the noble savage and the return to Nature then fashionable in Paris. After leaving Tahiti Bougainville determined to reach the unknown east coast of Australia,
and with his two ships he was better equipped for the
task than the English commanders had been. He
pressed far into the gulf between Queensland and New
Guinea and came near to the Great Barrier Reef. After
experiencing dreadful dangers he was glad to beat out
of what seemed to be a trap, and take the well-known
course round northern New Guinea. In doing so he
came to Carteret's New Ireland and picked up part of
a lead plate set up by that explorer a few months before.

These voyages were made to the accompaniment of
much public interest at home. In 1766 a free translation and expansion of de Brosses's work appeared in
Edinburgh under the title of *Terra Australis Cognita*,
with all the original arguments for the advantages of
southern expansion to France altered to apply to
Great Britain. During the same years a remarkable
projector was at work, who was in some respects a man
of the Renaissance born out of his time. This was
Alexander Dalrymple. He had been in the service of
the East India Company, and during many years in
Asiatic waters had collected and studied all available
information about the South Sea. At Madras he had

found a manuscript which revealed the voyage of Torres long before, in the strait between New Guinea and Australia; and at Manila, captured by a British expedition from India in 1762, further evidence of Torres Strait was obtained.[1] In the 'sixties Dalrymple was in England, still intent on his researches. He it was who first studied the Dieppe Atlas of 1542 in the Royal MSS. and discovered that the French cartographers of the Renaissance had depicted Eastern Australia as a 'Coste Dangereuse' fringed by a continuous reef. He gathered his results into a book, completed in 1767 and published two years later. It was the most forceful of all the presentations of the argument for Terra Australis Incognita, which, by Dalrymple's science, was shown to occupy virtually the whole of the space which had not yet been sailed over in the South Pacific—and some of that which had. Dalrymple was more than a student laying plans for men of action to follow. He was determined to be the man of action himself. History, to his mind, had still room for a Columbus, a man of faith and destiny, who should both ponder and execute. He was convinced that, given a ship and crew, he would find and exploit the world's greatest continent. Like Columbus he was not a professional seaman, and in that respect he was fatally unfitted to his time. The Renaissance would have made it no disqualification, but in the eighteenth century the King's ships had to be commanded by the King's officers.

The opportunity arose in 1768, when Wallis had come home with news of Tahiti, but nothing had been heard of Carteret. A transit of Venus, a rare astro-

---

[1] Until recent years it was believed, on the authority of Matthew Flinders, that Dalrymple first obtained evidence of Torres Strait from the Manila MS. But a writing of Dalrymple's now establishes that he had seen evidence at Madras before 1759. See Royal Australian Hist. Society, *Journal*, vol. xiii, 1927, pp. 55–6.

nomical event, was due to take place in the following year. It would be observable in far northern latitudes and also in the southern tropics, and Wallis reported that Tahiti offered a better chance of a cloudless sky than did Norway or Hudson Bay. The Royal Society and the Admiralty co-operated to plan an expedition to the Pacific, first to observe the transit and then to discover the southern continent. Dalrymple applied for the command, but the Admiralty rejected him. He was offered a place as a scientific observer, but that would not content him; he would go as the South Sea Columbus or not at all. Dalrymple was a man of courage and energy. He was also of eccentric temper and impossible to get on with. It was fortunate that the expedition sailed without him, although he himself remained for the rest of his long life a man with a huge, unsatisfied grievance. In his disappointment he was generous enough to furnish his supplanters with his yet unpublished researches, including the evidence he had found of the existence of Torres Strait. The Admiralty appointed to the command James Cook, a warrant officer commissioned for the occasion. Joseph Banks, Fellow of the Royal Society, went at the head of the scientific staff.

In this manner Cook came to the task which was to result in the solving of all the South Sea mysteries and was to establish his own position as the greatest of all the South Sea navigators. It fell to him in the ordinary way of duty and not by any agitation on his own part. He was already known as an accomplished cartographer and a man of sterling character, and for those reasons his superiors selected him. He lost no time in applying his powerful intellect to the mastery of all the known facts of the problem, and his professional skill to the equipment of a ship and crew more able than any that had previously approached it.

Cook sailed in August 1768, and proceeded by way of Cape Horn to Tahiti. In doing so he sailed over another large tract of Davis Land, and the idea of a continent existing near Chile was completely discredited. After observing the transit successfully Cook carried out his geographical instructions—to search for Terra Australis as far south as 40 degrees, and, failing its discovery, to go westwards to the unknown side of Tasman's New Zealand, and determine the nature of that country. The Admiralty's detailed instructions about procedure in Terra Australis Incognita bear a marked resemblance to those devised for Drake two hundred years earlier. The eighteenth century knew nothing whatever of the plans of the sixteenth, but it was a case of like circumstances producing like reactions—which is the clue to many British imperial policies. Cook went somewhat higher than 40 degrees, and saw no land. He then turned away for New Zealand, sighted once by Tasman, and never seen since. Tasman, it may be remembered, assumed it to be part of the continent. Cook occupied six months, not merely in settling that question, but in making a careful and substantially accurate survey of the coasts. In essentials the map of New Zealand, as we know it, resulted, where previously there had been only a name and a conjecture. Cook had now fulfilled his orders, but he had six months' stores in hand, and a crew in excellent health by reason of his strict hygienic discipline. He therefore sailed west again for the unknown east coast of Australia. Others had done that, but had changed their minds before reaching it. Cook was the first to see it. He coasted northwards, charting as he went, and escaping dreadful perils on the Great Barrier Reef. One section of his course, it is said, has never since been followed by any ship of size. Finally he proved in practice what Dalrymple had proved on paper, the existence of Torres Strait between New Guinea and Australia.[1]

The expedition came home with much to report; more new discovery, in fact, than had been made by any since Tasman, and detailed work of a bulk and accuracy never hitherto produced by any explorer in history. The unknown continent had been diminished but not entirely disproved, although it had now shrunk into such high latitudes as left little hope that it would be commercially valuable. Cook thought that one more voyage would settle the question, and in 1772 he set out on that voyage. In three years he sailed nearly 70,000 miles, much of it in unknown waters, and did very effectually settle the question. During the antarctic summers he pushed south until he reached the region of permanent ice, not only in the South Pacific, but all round the Southern Ocean. Behind that ice, he judged, there might be land, but it must be so covered as to be indistinguishable for practical purposes from the ice-floes themselves. In sum, he reduced Terra Australis Incognita to Antarctica. In the winters he retired to warmer latitudes, revisited New Zealand and Tahiti, and discovered or rediscovered numerous islands, some of them unknown since the period of Spanish activity and incorrectly located by the navigators of that earlier time. Poor Dalrymple heard these results with injured feelings, and it seemed almost as if he blamed Cook for the shattering of his continental dream. It was little satisfaction to him to know that if he had erred he had done so in good company.

After these two voyages the ancient mysteries of the

[1] A. Kitson's *Life of Cook*, London, 1907, is a good general authority. The voyages as narrated by Beaglehole (op. cit.) have the benefit of some evidence subsequently discovered. The portion of the first voyage which was on the Australian coast-line is followed more fully in G. A. Wood's *Discovery of Australia*.

South Sea were mysteries no more, and only details remained to be elucidated. Cook had yet a third and last voyage to make, but for a different purpose. In the North Pacific, Bering and the Russians had discovered Bering Strait early in the century, but the southern coasts of Alaska and those of California were still imperfectly examined. Cook's task was to see if they contained an opening leading through to Hudson Bay and so to the Atlantic—the North West Passage, approached from its Pacific side. He sailed in 1776 by way of the Cape and the South Sea, revisiting for the last time New Zealand and the islands where he was a familiar and respected figure. Then he crossed the equator, discovered the Sandwich Islands, and probed for the passage. In California and Alaska it was not to be found. He passed north through Bering Strait, coasting its American and Asiatic shores until stopped by ice. At the close of the summer season of 1778 he was still unsatisfied that everything possible had been done, and determined to try again after wintering in a warmer latitude. The result is known, the greatest tragedy of the eighteenth century to science and seamanship. On February 14, 1779, Cook, at the age of fifty and in the fullness of his powers, was killed in a sudden petty quarrel with the natives of Hawaii, who revered him as a god even as they struck him down.

With that event we may close our hasty survey of the exploration of the Pacific. When Cook died, all the outlines of the ocean were known, the sailing-tracks established, the more important islands charted. Almost at once, as three centuries earlier with the Atlantic, regular trade began, and colonization followed; and Pacific enterprise took its place among the great oversea developments which shaped the growth of our country in the century of fruition which followed.

VII

THE OCEANIC FACTOR IN THE SHAPING OF MODERN ENGLAND

BY the Restoration of 1660 national thought had accepted the promotion of oceanic trade as one of the prime objects of English policy. Indeed, in comparing the attitude of late Stuart and early Stuart governments to this interest, we are conscious that the Interregnum marks a transition from one world to another: it would have seemed as much out of character for Charles II to have allowed any step prejudicial to English trade as it would for Charles I to have pursued any policy beneficial to it. It is unlikely that long views and deeply prophetic reasoning accounted for the growing conviction that the new long-distance trades provided the most fruitful fields for English activity. There was no prescience of the industrial transformation that the future was to achieve. But on the immediate considerations patent to every observer there was foundation for what speedily became an agreed national policy. European standards of living were everywhere rising owing to the availability of increasing supplies of tropical commodities and the expansion of business facilitated by the growing volume of currency produced by the mines of the West. Wealth was therefore most rapidly to be attained by seizing a great share, a monopoly if possible, of the supply of the tropical output, and the profits of disposing of it in the European market. With the wealth so acquired went power, the sea-power that was both generated by the oceanic trades and indispensable to their maintenance. This simple doctrine for mercantile supremacy had been struggling for acceptance during the century before the Restoration and was in full practice during the century after it. Industry, while by no means backward in that century, appeared subordinate, the handmaid of commerce, and much mercantile profit was independent of home industry, arising from the sale of goods obtained from without. Then, as the eighteenth century progressed, the proportions and the emphasis began to change. Industry increased its pace and its output and the number of hands it employed. Long-distance commerce found its reward less in the direct resale of exotic wares to European consumers and more in the provision of raw material for English industry, not only material for manufacture, such as cotton, but foods and stimulants, such as sugar and tea, to keep going the increasing population of operatives. And, having achieved this function, commerce had then to distribute the manufactured results over the world. Thus, well before the early nineteenth century opened the roles were reversed, and commerce became the handmaid of industry. That immense quickening of industrial activity, which it is now unfashionable to call the Industrial Revolution, produced the world in which we live to-day. What produced the quickening itself? There are various approaches to that question, and one of them is by way of oceanic enterprise. By following one clear sequence of developments—with an emphatic proviso that it is not exclusive of other sequences—we may regard the industrial age as a fruit of the enterprise set going by Columbus and Henry the Navigator.

We take up the story in the mid-seventeenth century, after England had outlived her period of apprenticeship and tentative experiment and had simplified her doctrine to the seizure and exploitation of the greatest possible share in the oceanic trades. The rivals actually in possession of the greatest share were the Dutch, and they accordingly were the first enemies in the mercantile struggle. Cromwell, a moderate man, and hampered also, as a mercantilist might have put it, by religious motives, had been willing to share equally with the Dutch while extirpating everyone else; and his conclusion of the first Dutch war had been on moderate terms, the English regaining the trade of their own possessions into which the Dutch had intruded, but not depriving the Dutch of anything that was legitimately theirs.

Restoration England took a harder tone. Its sentiment was for smashing the Dutch and achieving monopoly. A sea-captain said to Pepys: 'The trade of the world is too little for us two, therefore one must down.'[1] It was a private man's remark, but it expressed the public view. But the second Dutch war, and still more the third, failed to achieve the necessary obliteration, and England had to be content with improving her share. She did so very markedly with the unwitting aid of France; for after England made her final Dutch peace in 1674, Louis XIV continued for four years more his attempts to invade and conquer the United Provinces, and the Dutch were so weakened that England seized more of their trade than she had won by her own naval efforts. France also lost ground, and the promising work of Colbert was neutralized by his master's military ambitions. It is roughly true that England's foreign trade was doubled in the reign of Charles II. Some of that increase was due to the Navigation Acts, but some also to the waste of her rivals' strength by the acts of Louis XIV.

In the wars with France that began in 1689 political motives were obvious, but they were interlinked with mercantile. In the conditions of that time great mili-

[1] *Diary*, Feb. 2, 1664.

tary efforts were incompatible with mercantile success, if only because they placed in control of the state persons who had little sympathy with commercial aims. Naval efforts, on the other hand, were of direct help to trade, since they consisted largely in its protection and in destroying the shipping of rivals. England played for naval supremacy and sent comparatively few of her own men to fight on land, and was rewarded by making the Peace of Utrecht in the character of the acknowledged greatest sea-power, a character that she long retained. So began the Hanoverian period, with Great Britain in a position to exploit still farther her mercantile advance.

There are a great number of scattered statistics available on the growth of oceanic trade in the eighteenth century, but no complete and systematic conspectus. The figures themselves may be highly misleading unless allowance is made for factors not always apparent. A parliamentary return of 1803,[1] for example, while stating that the year's exports amounted nominally to £33,000,000, of which £22,000,000 represented British manufactures, bears an appended note that the true value of those British manufactures was £40,000,000, since the customs were levied on values arbitrarily fixed by the book of rates of 1696, more than a century out of date. It is a warning against implicit faith in statistics, and there are many such qualifications to be made, for much trade followed indirect routes, and goods coming apparently from one country had often originated in another. The best use of the figures is therefore the cautious deduction of tendencies, sufficiently broadly stated to make some allowance for unknown errors.

[1] P.R.O., T 64/273–89, No. 9. The number of the volume of documents is *one* of 273–89. I regret that I did not make a correct note when consulting the MS. at the Record Office. It is now (January, 1941) not possible to remedy the deficiency.

One such general statement which appears entirely justifiable is that, just as trade had doubled in value during the Restoration period, so, even allowing for a continuous fall in money values, it continued afterwards to grow at a much faster rate than did the country's population. Throughout the eighteenth century the mercantile wealth of Great Britain expanded rapidly and continuously and, had the increase been reasonably well distributed, every class in the community would have been in easier circumstances at the century's close than at its opening. And, again very broadly and with some large exceptions, this general increase in well-being was a fact. Although birth-rates probably did not rise, death-rates certainly fell, and from about the middle of the century the population increased at a more rapid rate than ever before. In other words, the expectation of life became longer. Some of the credit, although by no means all, must be accorded to the amenities made more general by the growth of foreign trade.

Economists agreed that the oceanic trades contributed more to the growth of national wealth than did the more local commerce with the continent of Europe. It was an underlying assumption of much economic literature that the trade of Europe was relatively fixed in amount while that of the outer world was capable of great expansion in the hands of a dominant sea-power. Sir William Davenant in the late seventeenth century attributed the increase of wealth in his time to the Colonial, East Indian, and European trades in the respective proportions of nine, six, and five.[1] It was, of course, extremely difficult to make any such computation, since much of our European trade consisted in the disposal of goods of colonial origin. By the early years of George III, on the eve of the great

[1] E. Lipson, *Economic History of England*, iii. 209–10.

industrial expansion, we were importing rather more
from the Atlantic colonies and the East Indies than
from Europe, but exporting nearly twice as much to
Europe as to trans-oceanic markets, with a net favourable balance of nearly £3,000,000 a year.[1] This forms
an illustration of the gains achieved mainly by the
exploitation of tropical commodities, pursued whole-
heartedly since the Restoration. Shortly afterwards,
as has been said, the emphasis began to fall more
markedly on increasing manufactures and their sale to
all the world.

That the oceanic trade was mainly in tropical or
sub-tropical wares is sufficiently evident. The return
of 1765[2] shows a total colonial and Eastern trade of
£9,000,000, of which only 1½ millions was with the
American colonies north of Maryland (and some of
that probably in West Indian produce). At least five-
sixths, therefore, of that year's oceanic trade was in
the buying and selling of plantation and East Indian
commodities. The Atlantic plantations at that time
accounted for twice as much trade as the East Indies,
but the East Indian proportion increased during the
remainder of the century. By 1798 it was about double
that of the plantations. This extremely rapid advance
in the India and China interest was a factor of great
importance in the national development.

We have now to consider the effects of these external
activities upon the condition of England itself. In the
first place, they undoubtedly increased the fund of fluid
capital available for investment in industry. As before,
there are no comprehensive statistics, but what there
are point to an extremely rapid increase in mobile
wealth. Mercantile fortunes became ever greater and
more numerous until, in the mid-eighteenth century,
the millionaire who had made his money in business

[1] P.R.O., same volume as noted above, No. 1.   [2] Ibid.

appeared as a new social phenomenon. The plantation trades first produced these rich men, and especially the West Indian sugar plantations, many of which were owned by persons resident in England. The East Indian trade, in its early days decried by the over-simple bullionist doctrine for its export of silver in return for luxuries, speedily showed that it was a maker and not a spender of the national wealth. The profits which it made by the re-export of its cargoes far exceeded its shipments of coin to the East. After the conquest of Bengal and the domination of the Carnatic, the fruits of Clive's victories, Indian profits made a gigantic leap upwards, for they were no longer the profits of trade alone, but of government also. For centuries Europe had been sending silver to the East, and substantial amounts of it had accumulated in the treasuries of Indian rulers. When the English became rulers some of these hoards were unlocked. Clive alone made a quarter of a million by a single transaction, the enthronement of Mir Jaffier; and there were many others. The era of the nabobs set in, of the home-coming Anglo-Indians whose wealth became a social and political force in the reign of George III. The total extent of that wealth was grossly exaggerated by observers, but the reality was nevertheless considerable.

It appears that this process did not involve the retransference of specie from Asia to Great Britain. The nabob did not bring his fortune home with him in cash, for the sufficient reason that silver was worth more in the East than in Europe. The effect was less simply attained, but none the less certainly. The old process had been for the Company to export silver, obtain commodities, and sell them in Europe for yet greater amounts of silver, which came from the Spanish mines in the West. After Plassey, although the inflow of Eastern goods grew greater than ever before, the outflow of silver from England virtually ceased: the goods were being bought with money already in Asia and now made available for trade. It is computed that in this manner some fifteen million pounds were retained in England which would otherwise have gone out to fertilize the Eastern trade, while all the profits of that trade were kept and enlarged.[1] The retiring nabob drew bills on London and cashed them when he reached home. The Company received Indian revenues and laid them out in Asiatic goods. Indian wares alone did not absorb the whole investment. The China trade, long precarious, entered on its first phase of great expansion after the middle of the century, and in that phase the China goods were largely paid for with Indian silver. Some two thousand tons of China tea were legally imported in 1762, and seven thousand in 1790, besides great quantities known to have been smuggled by devious operations largely financed by English capital.[2] In sum, the Indian conquests enabled vastly increased returns to be secured from Asiatic trade, while the European money that would otherwise have been invested in that trade was retained in England and added to her stock of fluid wealth.

The simple system by which English merchants were to act as middlemen for the sale of tropical commodities to continental Europe did not continue uncomplicated for very long. Most of the oceanic goods were in one sense or another raw materials, and so provided employment in England in preparing them for the market. Tobacco, the first of the plantation crops, seems not to have been important in this respect, but sugar, which succeeded it, needed to undergo many processes to render it fit for sale. In the early

[1] J. M. Holzman, *The Nabobs in England*, New York, 1926, pp. 88–9.
[2] C. F. Mullett, *The British Empire*, London, 1938, pp. 219–20.

stages the planters themselves sought to do this work,
but it quickly became a specialized task for refineries
of the factory type, and was removed from the plantations to England. Bristol and London were building
sugar-works before the close of the seventeenth century,
and it was stated that every colonist in Barbados or
Jamaica gave employment to four persons at home.[1]
Cotton was another raw material which was obviously
important in this respect. At the beginning of the
eighteenth century about 450 tons of raw cotton were
imported in a year; in other words, the cargoes of two
or three average merchantmen. By 1750 this amount
was trebled, and by 1780 more than trebled again.
Then the really huge increase set in. In 1800 the
annual import was 25,000 tons of raw cotton, and in
1810 nearly 60,000 tons; and so forward. Other raw
materials increasingly available were dyestuffs both
from the East and from the West, gums and oils from
the African coast, whale oil and kindred products from
fisheries continuously expanding and changing their
location, and beaver furs from all the frontier regions
of North America. Whale oil was indispensable for
many manufacturing uses, and the opening of the
Pacific provided a vast new area of supply which was
being vigorously exploited within a few years of the
death of Captain Cook.

Side by side with the increasing flood of raw material
imported there went the expansion of markets for
exports. In this matter the oceanic trades produced a
radical change in the thought and practice of Europe.
By a theory which tended to lag behind the advance
of the facts, the trade of Europe was considered in the
sixteenth century, and even in the seventeenth, to be
stationary in amount, and not expanding. It seemed
that there was a given population, with a given volume

[1] Ibid., p. 214.

of wants and of purchasing power with which to satisfy them. The mercantile nations competed with one another for the largest shares of this finite amount of trade, and it was commonly believed that one nation's profit necessarily implied another nation's loss. So, in the seventeenth century, when these ideas were most clearly enunciated, the game of beggar-my-neighbour was unsparingly played, and commerce was pursued as a species of warfare. Colbert elaborated a great system to recover for France the share which the slackness of his predecessors had omitted to claim. The English tried to ruin the Dutch and the French impartially, and were even bitterly resentful when their Scottish fellow subjects sought to become a mercantile nation under the inspiration of William Paterson. Before the inauguration of oceanic trade there was much truth in these premisses, and for some time afterwards they were regarded as true. Nevertheless, oceanic trade did increase the internal trade of Europe by creating new wants, a phenomenon that was instantly observable but was long in securing recognition. The spices, tobacco, sugar, coffee, tea, rum, porcelain constituted such new wants when once the taste for them had been stimulated, and the cotton fabrics of India are an outstanding example. To supply these things was an evident business for the oceanic trader, but the effect went farther. Some of them, or good substitutes for them, could be supplied by Europe's own craftsmen, once the desire had been created, and so the purely local trade of Europe became less stationary and visibly expanded as a result of the oceanic stimulus. This, and most notably in the instance of the cotton manufacture, accounts for a good proportion of the increasing industry of England in the eighteenth century.

The purely oceanic aspect of the expansion of markets for home industry had been obvious from the outset. Hakluyt and all the Tudor propagandists insisted that oceanic enterprise would be the means by which the unemployed of England would be 'set on work', supplying entirely new markets additional to those of stationary Europe. The opening of the North East Passage would yield a sale of cloth to the people of Tartary, and that of the North West to the red men of North America. Those particular hopes proved illusory, but in other directions Elizabethan England made a beginning. The African traders sold miscellaneous manufactures to the Moors of Barbary and the negroes of the Gold Coast, while slaves were not the only wares carried by John Hawkins and his imitators to the Spanish Main. In their small way these adventurers stimulated English industry. Stuart England founded the colonies but, forgetting the teaching of Hakluyt, valued them almost exclusively as sources of supply of profitable wares. Barbados under Charles II was 'the principal pearl in His Majesty's crown' mainly because its sugar gave employment to English refineries and profit to English middlemen, and much less because it consumed English manufactures, although in fact it did so. New England, not yielding a lucrative import, ranked as no pearl at all, but an annoying encumbrance.

The colonies, indeed, in their first century were but small consumers, for there were not many colonists, and most of them lived a rough and brutish life devoid of the amenities which English industry could have supplied. But in the eighteenth century their numbers grew. In 1688, taking America and the West Indies together, there were probably 350,000 inhabitants of the Atlantic possessions, including negro slaves.[1] England and Wales at that time contained about 5½

[1] *Cambr. Hist. of the Brit. Empire,* vol. i, p. 267.

millions, so that the colonial population was roughly one-fifteenth that of the mother country, and possessed a rather low standard of wants. Those wants, such as they were, and so far as they involved import of goods, had all to be supplied by the mother country under the operation of the Laws of Trade, but the stimulus to home industry was not yet great. By 1760 the total colonial population had risen to about 2 millions, while that of England was about 7 millions, and the proportion was thus nearly one-third. Moreover, the colonists were becoming more luxurious and consumed more manufactured goods in relation to their numbers. Here indeed was a new market, and a rapidly expanding one, for American population was doubling itself every twenty years. The monopoly of supplying it was lost in the War of Independence, but yet a good share was retained, for the citizen of the United States continued to purchase voluntarily where the subject of George III had dealt under compulsion. There were other colonial populations, Spanish and Portuguese, partly supplied by English manufacturers. Much trade went on with Spanish America legitimately through Spain, and some illegitimately by the operations of the smugglers who caused the War of Jenkins' Ear. A series of treaties with Portugal, from the reign of Charles I to that of Anne, secured entry for English goods into Brazil and the Portuguese islands. East of the Cape of Good Hope the expansion of markets was less rapid, but with growing range and experience the East India Company did more in this respect than it had done in the seventeenth century.

Accumulations of capital seeking profitable investment, increasing supplies of raw material, expanding markets for the disposal of manufactured goods—these factors inevitably stimulated English industry. Whether they were the fundamental causes of our modern industrialization, or whether they merely assisted and quickened a process of independent origin, are questions incapable of absolute proof, since the statistics are incomplete and the intricacies of cause and effect too involved to be unravelled. But we can observe contemporary opinions and some of the phenomena, and derive impressions which probably contain some of the truth.

Modern research has corrected the idea that an industrial revolution, involving a complete change of methods, set in suddenly in the early years of George III. We now know that the change from independent domestic craftsmanship to factory work under capitalist control had been slowly proceeding for more than a hundred years before that time, and that industry had been employing a steadily increasing proportion of the nation as compared with trade and agriculture. With the weakening of the 'revolutionary' conception of the process, a cause which used to be regarded as a sufficient explanation for it recedes into the background. We can no longer account for a supposed sudden revolution as having been directly occasioned by a sudden crop of mechanical inventions — spinning-jennies, power-looms, steam-engines, and the like. These inventions are now appearing rather as effects of quickened industry than as originating causes. They were such as could have been made at any time after the mid-seventeenth century, and would have been made, had the demand existed; and as soon as the mid-eighteenth century made the demand, they came rapidly into being. The eighteenth century certainly made that demand. In its last forty years there was a remarkable and progressive intensification of industry. Old manufactures increased their output, and new ones were inaugurated, and the machines were invented as required, not for doing things that had never been done before, but for quickening processes that had long been performed by slower means. It is clear that the machines did not cause the industrial energy. We must look to earlier and more widespread stimuli.

The cotton trade, which was the first and greatest of the new industries, yields some suggestions. In the Restoration period imported Indian cotton fabrics found a ready sale, and began to oust woollen cloth from some of its uses. The cloth-makers complained, and in 1700 obtained a legal prohibition of the use of Indian cottons, a prohibition which was strengthened in 1721. The prohibition was less effective than the cloth industry desired, since it did not extend to the introduction of Indian fabrics for re-export. It had also the unexpected result of the beginning of a cotton manufacture in England by persons whose conduct the clothiers described as despicable and unpatriotic. Cotton wool had been imported from the West Indies since the earliest days of colonization, but it had been used mainly as a quilting material and not as a textile, and the demand had been limited. English manufacturers now began to experiment with cotton cloth, and Defoe in 1727 noted that Manchester was already a busy centre of the manufacture. The original importation of Indian chintzes and muslins had created a new want which insisted on being satisfied in spite of legal prohibitions. An investigator has concluded that 'the seeds of the cotton industry were in fact brought to England in the ships of the East India Company'.[1] Most of the output for the first fifty years went overseas to Africa, the West Indies, and the plantations of America, where it was more acceptable than woollen cloth, and helped to purchase increased supplies of tropical products. But it seems that in spite of the law

[1] Paul Mantoux, *The Industrial Revolution in the Eighteenth Century*, London, 1928, p. 107.

cottons were worn in England long before the repeal
of the restriction in 1774, for there are records of street
riots raised by unemployed clothiers against women
dressed in the forbidden fabric.

Both the market and the material for the cotton
manufacture were thus of oceanic origin, and so also
was the money which financed the early business. The
north of England had always been poorer and rougher
in its standards of living than the south, and the new
commodities supplied by the ocean trades were distinctly later in coming into use in the north. But
towards the end of the seventeenth century development began. Liverpool was by nature the best port of
entry for Atlantic-borne cargoes, and its trade grew
important by the supply of tobacco and sugar and
minor West Indian produce. Liverpool thus became
an oceanic port, where previously its trade had been
chiefly with Ireland. Its shipowners early perceived
the profits to be made in the slave trade, in which they
specialized and cut into the existing supremacy of
Bristol. In the eighteenth century Liverpool grew rich
on all the colonial trades, not only importing for the
northern market, but re-exporting and acting as a
carrier. The total tonnage in and out of the port in
1710 was 27,000, and by 1770 it was 140,000, a five-
fold increase in sixty years; and the population of the
town was multiplied in the same proportion. Capital
was consequently amassed, and it was applied to the
utilization of the raw cotton brought in from the West
Indies and Brazil. The figures show clearly that the
growth of Liverpool antedated the rise of the Lancashire cotton industry, and an investigator of the subject
has no doubt of the connexion between them. 'The
growth of Lancashire', he says, 'depended first of all
on the development of Liverpool and her trade.'[1]

[1] Mantoux, op. cit., pp. 109–11.

That statement applies to the origins and localization of the cotton manufacture, but it is not to be supposed that when cotton became important it depended solely on locally won capital. Cotton began to grow gigantic in the last quarter of the century, and attracted the mobile capital of the country at large. Strict proof is impossible, but there is a significant suggestion that Clive's Indian conquests, causing a temporary cessation of the drain of silver from England, not only set free a fund of cash for industrial enterprise but largely accounted for the expansion of credit that also played its part.

Another aspect of the bearing of the long-distance commerce upon the new industrialism may also be illustrated by cotton, although here again exact statement is unwarranted, but reasonable inference can be drawn. In its first half-century cotton was manufactured primarily for export to the tropics, the home market being subsidiary and hampered by restrictions. The vendor of goods to the other side of the world was necessarily a capitalist, for he had to wait long for the return of his investment. To conduct his business economically and to maintain his distant connexions he needed his goods to be available in bulk, of uniform quality and price, and he required also to be sure of repeating his shipments without violent fluctuation in those respects. These conditions would not have been fulfilled by the old-style domestic manufacture, with its sudden variations in price and output interlinked with agricultural considerations and the chances of the summer's weather, and complicated by local differences in the fashion of craftsmanship. To collect a shipload of textiles from such producers was a wasteful and uncertain process. The long-distance trade virtually dictated the system of the large factory, with its labour on fixed wages and its output predictable in advance.

Cotton, the export industry, became such a factory trade early in its history; and, however regrettable, it seems unavoidable to see in the audacity, enterprise, and individualism of the oceanic adventurers an agent in creating the drab industrial uniformity of modern urban life. Wool, a more ancient manufacture, its domestic methods rooted in the medieval past, and its disposal made in smaller parcels to home and European markets, resisted the change for a generation after cotton had shown the way; but wool also had ultimately to submit to factory discipline.

On its much smaller scale the pottery manufacture clearly shows the action of the same forces. English pottery before the latter part of the eighteenth century was poor stuff, roughly made of bad material, and not even evincing the artistic qualities associated with so many domestic handicrafts. The stimulus came from China in the cargoes of the East Indiamen. Chinese porcelain was an object of delight before the close of the Stuart period, and William III's Queen Mary was an ardent collector. But it was too rare and costly for use even by the rich, and silver and pewter served the well-to-do English table for half a century to come. Yet a want had been created, and in due time it was supplied, primarily by the enterprise of Josiah Wedgwood. His manufacture was something entirely new, factory-organized and capitalist to the core, located where there was a population of poor domestic craftsmen, but drilling them into better ways by Wedgwood's high standards, transporting superior raw material from Cornwall, agitating for improved communications between the factories and the sea, and overcoming the difficulties of carrying such fragile stuff to markets near and far. England quickly gave up pewter for the cheaper, cleaner, and more pleasant-looking Staffordshire ware, and yet another modern industry was firmly established. The long-distance merchantmen aided it with a new and expanding market, for at that juncture the prospering Americans were welcoming household amenities. The older colonists had eaten from wooden platters carved by the users, but enterprising Liverpool brought them the new glazed earthenware, and they bought it in bulk.

Birmingham and its surrounding district of metalworkers provides an epitome of the changes with which we are dealing. From the outset the tropical traders had laded metal goods for climates in which English cloth could expect no sale. Fire-arms, knives and hatchets, copper kettles, pewter bowls and dishes, nails and chains, brass ornaments, buttons and trinkets, these things tempted the African to part with his ivory, gold dust and palm-oil, and his fellow African captives; they bought beaver-skins from the hunting Indian of North America; some of them appealed to the white colonists of the plantations, and some even to the cultured East Indian and the fastidious Chinaman. The Brummagem country discovered certain local advantages which enabled it to specialize in the supply, and early developed a population of skilled metalworkers. The eighteenth-century expansion capitalized it and organized it in factories, and Matthew Boulton's Soho works, featuring James Watt's improved steam-engines, became one of the standard entertainments for distinguished sightseers. Birmingham, of course, enjoyed a pre-eminent home and European market, but its capitalistic expansion was hastened by the mercantile wealth won in distant trades and by the demand of those trades for shipments in bulk.

In ascribing the industrialization of England so largely to the effects of her oceanic commerce, we are obliged to take notice of the fact that other oceanic powers were not similarly affected. The Dutch come instantly to mind as a case in point. But their great mercantile profits were won by the process most evident in England at the time of the Restoration, the sale to all Europe of tropical goods, and by their services as efficient sea-carriers of other nations' goods. The Dutch were not great producers, and their industries were not ready to be revolutionized. Their country lacked coal and iron, and their enormous capital gains were seriously depleted by the necessities for frontier fortification and military defence. The terrible French wars of the period 1672 to 1713 gravely and permanently weakened the Dutch people. By the time the industrial age was ready to set in, their wealth and energy had long receded, and they had become a minor power with memories of past greatness.

Still less had Spain the makings of an industrial country. In the days of her imperial greatness her energies were military, and in greatness and decline alike she was always financially impoverished. It is one of the paradoxes of modern history that, while Spain produced in her colonies the precious metals that expanded capital and credit in all Europe, she herself was always on the verge of bankruptcy and had never the wherewithal to vitalize her industries. Of Portugal in this respect little need be said. Early empire-building diminished and diluted her population, and there was never any basis of industry to which her trading wealth might have been applied. In all the later period the trade of the Portuguese empire was in effect British, and its industrial effects were seen in Great Britain and not in Portugal.

France requires closer examination, for she remained a great and vigorous power when the industrial age was beginning. In spite of all the losses of the eighteenth-century wars the French colonial trade was as great as the British in 1789, and the East Indian trade was still considerable. In the West Indies, where mercantile wealth was made, the French interest was predominant. Hayti was a much greater and more productive colony than Jamaica, while Guadeloupe was richer than all the English Lesser Antilles together, and Martinique came not far behind it. France also had thriving domestic manufactures with which she supplied the export needs of her colonial trade. What then was lacking to produce the result seen in England, the large-scale organization of industry? The answer seems to lie in the constitution and politics of Bourbon France. Taxation was heavy and inequitable, and the merchant classes paid more than their share. Arbitrary government caused a lack of the confidence essential to industrial ventures; there was no banking system to render capital fluid and mobile; the Frenchman had no Bill of Rights to defend his wealth against the state. Thus, although France possessed the long-distance markets, and some access to raw materials, and her people produced a sufficiency of craftsmen and inventors, free capital was lacking in the form so evident in England. Perhaps also an arithmetical factor had its weight. With approximately equal volumes of oceanic trade, the French home population was some 20 millions when the English was 7 millions. The reaction of colonial trade upon home industry was therefore more blunted in France, the demand for export cargoes more widely spread, and the insistence upon factory supplies for the long-distance trades not nearly so urgent. And then, in the closing decade of the century, when in spite of all deterrents there were signs of a nascent industrialization in France, there came the most prolonged war of modern times, in which the national energy went all into militarism, and sea-borne trade was disorganized by blockade.

To round off this somewhat discursive survey of the

causes of English industrialization, we may revert again
to fluid capital as the indispensable factor. The Bank
of England, closely allied with the great oceanic companies, began the work of concentrating private men's
capital and enabling it to be applied with confidence
to new businesses; and later in the eighteenth century
smaller banks sprang up all over the country, conducted
often by successful merchants, to increase the contacts
between commerce and manufacture. A recent writer
on the old colonial empire has stated his conclusion
that the Industrial Revolution 'was directly although
not entirely traceable to overseas factors'.[1] A leading
authority on our economic history remarks that,
'speaking generally, the capital which found its way
into manufactures was drawn, in this country, not
from rents but from trade'.[2] Burke in 1786, debating
the French commercial treaty of that year, declared:
'our capital gives us a superiority which enables us to
set all the efforts of France to rival our manufactures
at defiance: the powers of capital are irresistible in
trade.' And Burke at least had well-known views on
the East Indian source of much of that capital.

During the first generation of the intensive changes
in industry occurred the loss of the American colonies
and the long war with revolutionary France. These
events caused careful reconsideration of imperial policy,
an examination of which will show that the oceanic
interest remained of prime importance. That interest,
having largely created the new industry, had now to
sustain it. The long-distance trades had become the
handmaids of the factories.

The contemporary view of the independence of
America has often been misinterpreted in more recent
times. Accustomed to a world-map on which large
and valuable areas are coloured red, we are apt to

[1] Mullett, op. cit., p. 214.   [2] Lipson, op. cit., vol. iii, p. 208.

assume that the loss of the greatest of those areas existing in the eighteenth century, with the most advanced colonial population up to that time founded, must have been regarded as a crippling disaster. On the map it looks as though the secession of the United States knocked the heart out of the colonial empire, leaving little but fringes and fragments as the monuments of an adventure that had failed. For many decades, so the theory runs, England turned her back upon imperial expansion until very gradually, and in a humble, dejected spirit, such activities revived of their own motion in the middle nineteenth century. Such a view is implicit in a standard late-Victorian work like Egerton's *History of British Colonial Policy*, which implies unmistakably that for forty years there was no policy; for it jumps in one page from 1783 to 1823.[1]

More recent research has shown that this view is unjustified, that there was no hiatus, and that if for 'colonial' we read 'oceanic'—a difference of emphasis—the period after the Treaties of Versailles was one of activity and confidence. The history of that period has not yet been adequately written, but enough is known to enable a brief provisional description to be given here.

There was indeed some heartbreak over the American defeat: almost literally Chatham's heart broke in contemplation of the prospect; but it was not unmixed in less idealistic minds with prudent calculations of some accompanying advantages. The men of the eighteenth century were not for the most part imperialists of the modern type, regarding expansion as national self-expression in the lofty ideals of freedom, good government, and humanitarianism. They looked much more directly to profit expressed in the concrete terms of growing trade and industry. The American

[1] The reference is to the original edition, 1897.

colonists had never easily fitted into the scheme of the mercantile empire. Their own contribution to the growth of British wealth had been a minor consideration, offset by their competition with the mother country in the exploitation of the more lucrative tropics. To some hard thinkers it appeared a positive advantage that the Americans had withdrawn, and might henceforward be excluded as foreigners from participation in the rich business that yet remained under the flag. We are accustomed perhaps to accord too exclusive weight to the Whig denunciations of tyranny and hatred of George III in accounting for the half-heartedness of the effort to put down the American revolt. We should not forget also the undercurrent of opinion that, as a matter of cold calculation, American subjection was not worth fighting for.

From 1783 onwards there was indeed an active imperial policy, although it was not directed to the creation of another United States by the settlement of large numbers of white colonists in a temperate climate. The development of British provinces in Canada forms an exception to this statement, but it is accounted for by the fact that Great Britain owed a debt of honour to the Loyalists of the old American colonies. They were suffering for their faithfulness to the losing side, and accommodation had to be found for them in Nova Scotia, New Brunswick, and Ontario. The policy preferred was that of strengthening the British hold upon all the tropical trading areas and of acquiring, when opportunity arose, naval bases and ports of call for merchantmen on the great oceanic routes.

The West Indies were still the richest area of the Atlantic. Their volume of trade depended almost directly upon the quantity of field-labour they could command, and in the years after the peace, in spite of the humanitarian protest that was arising in England, slaves were transported from Africa in greater numbers than ever before; and the sugar output grew accordingly. The islands had always had a close connexion with the Northern American mainland, which had taken their sugar and molasses and supplied them with foodstuffs. Now that the mainland was no longer British, this intercourse was forbidden by the Laws of Trade. By the principles of the Navigation Acts a cargo for a foreign country had to be consigned to England and there transhipped. But this rule had been made with European countries only in view, and it was absurd to require West Indian produce to cross the Atlantic twice in order to reach the United States. An Order in Council therefore permitted direct intercourse, but limited it to trade in British ships: independent Americans were not to sail under their own flag to the West Indies. The order continued unrelaxed for over a dozen years. It was a strain upon human nature, and there were many infringements with the connivance of the island planters. Readers of Southey's *Life of Nelson* will remember that Nelson as a young captain showed all his customary zeal in arresting intruding American vessels, and got into hot water with his superiors, who were inclined to wink at the illicit traffic.

Yet more important than the monopoly of the sugar trade was the finding of markets for the new factory industries. A direct trade with Spanish America had tempted English enterprise since the days of Elizabeth. Smuggling and interloping had sometimes flourished and sometimes been checked, but, apart from the concession of one shipload of traffic a year by the Treaty of Utrecht, the Spanish government had never permitted it in principle. The Utrecht concession had worked badly and had been annulled. The interlopers were the cause of the war with Spain in 1739, and the British operations in that war were directed to prising open the locked-up South American trade. They failed, but in one form or another the project remained in the minds of strategists until it was realized with the independence of Latin America, achieved with British help and patronage in the 1820's. In the post-1783 period the method of approach was to permit Spanish intercourse with the British West Indies. It is interesting as showing how even a sacred principle of the Navigation Acts could be jettisoned on the new overriding demand for markets.

The West African trade offered a minor market for a variety of manufactures, and British policy did not neglect it. Slaves had long ceased to be obtained by white men raiding along the coast. The coastal tribes were now for the most part in alliance with the slave-traders, and supplied them by capturing the remoter inland people. In the generation before its prohibition in 1807 the slave-trade increased in volume, as did the export of goods with which payment was made; and even after 1807 British slaving went on under the Portuguese and Spanish flags, and the market for manufactures to some extent existed. A powerful element in British affairs was, however, determined to put down slaving. For police purposes it desired to maintain the British influence on the coast, and the trend of development was to promote all innocuous forms of African intercourse. The vegetable products were increasingly valuable to industry, and here the mercantile and humanitarian interests coincided. In Africa, as in the West Indies, there was no thought of relinquishing empire after 1783, but a very active study of its promotion. The establishment of the Sierra Leone colony for freed slaves in 1787 and the abortive proposal to transport British convicts to West Africa at the same time are illustrations of the new imperialism in which new motives mingled with the older search for profit.

In the East the new industrial mercantilism was extraordinarily active. Warren Hastings and Lord Cornwallis introduced order among the Company's servants and better government in Bengal. The preservation of British interests in India seemed, and was, a more important result of the War of Independence than the loss of the American colonies. English public opinion was intensely interested in these questions, and the struggles over Fox's India Bill and Pitt's India Act overshadowed all other political transactions. The subsequent Indian wars up to 1805 brought great territories under British control. The Company received their revenues and became the governing agency, while trading interests expanded beyond the limit at which its monopoly could be maintained. The way was thus prepared for the throwing open of the Indian trade by the revised charter of 1813.

The greatest developments, however, were taking place farther East, and here the Company was able to retain its position for a further twenty years. Its ships and those of the so-called country traders, many of them British, entered the Eastern Archipelago in force after 1783 and passed through to China. The European demand for tea was insatiable, and by the close of the century the annual traffic at Canton was running into millions. For a period after Clive's time Indian silver was the chief purchaser of China goods, and from 1790 Indian opium came into prominence. British manufactures played an increasing part, but other commodities had to be brought in. The newly opened Pacific made its contribution. Cook in his last voyage had made a hasty survey of the coast of California, and the China merchants seized upon the fact that it yielded in the furs of the sea-otter a product that China desired. From 1785 there existed a settlement for their collection at Nootka Sound, and ships regularly crossed from

California to China. Spanish objection to this far-western British outpost led to the Nootka Sound crisis of 1790, a somewhat parallel transaction to the Falklands affair of twenty years before. As on the earlier occasion, the British government was prepared to fight, and Spain gave way. When sea-otter declined in importance the islands of the Western Pacific were brought into the orbit of the China trade, for their sandalwood was a much-prized commodity. British collectors of sandalwood began to work from the new convict colony at Sydney, and were active in the Fiji group as early as 1804. The sandalwood trade for the Chinese market had a life of more than fifty years, until it was virtually ended by the exhaustion of supplies.

In the last two decades of the eighteenth century British world trade was growing at a rate which may be described as feverish in comparison with anything that the past could show. Behind it, both stimulated by it and stimulating it to greater efforts, was British manufacturing industry, continually expanding and continually demanding expansion of markets. In this delicately balanced, or perhaps unbalanced, condition the country plunged into the twenty-two years of war with Revolutionary France. The stakes were higher than in any previous conflict. Defeat in earlier wars would have meant loss of pride and prestige and superfluous colonial wealth, perhaps change of dynasty, and the ruin of many individuals of the ruling and mercantile classes. Defeat in this war would have brought economic collapse, the starvation of millions, political and social revolution. Oceanic enterprise and its domestic consequences had produced this vulnerable position, but they were now to prove that they had produced the means of defending it. Three of those means may be enumerated: the most efficient fighting fleet the world has seen, its sea-talent as well as its

material having common origin with those of the innu-
merable merchant fleets that traversed every ocean;
an elastic and expanding wealth, ill-distributed, no
doubt, but unprecedented in bulk and resilience to
disaster; and a tradition of statesmanship, an instinctive
strategy, guiding even mediocre men to do the right
thing, bred from two centuries of familiarity with the
whole earth as a field of play, and proving able after
anxious years to use the sea-power and the wealth to
overcome the greatest military ascendancy that continental Europe had produced. The result needs no
description here, and the methods have been more
widely studied than the means. Sea-power and sea-
talent in their widest senses, embracing not only
fighting men but merchant seamen, merchants, finan-
ciers and ministers, and an understanding of issues
widespread among the people at large, won the
Napoleonic War. Our trade with Europe was hampered and partly stopped, but our trade with all the
rest of the world increased during the struggle and held
its position afterwards. The blockade, carried out by
virtue of sea-power, assured something approaching a
monopoly of the ocean routes, and so disorganized
continental business that no imitation of British industrial methods could be attempted for a full generation.
Finally, this use of sea-power enabled our small land-
power to achieve disproportionately great results, and
Wellington and his handful of heroes could thrust home
their point in the vital spot with a smaller expenditure
of blood than has ever attended the overthrow of an
empire. The Napoleonic War was the first of the
desperate all-or-nothing struggles characteristic of
modern civilization. That of 1914 was the second, and
very differently handled; and now the third proceeds.

To the threshold of the nineteenth century is as far
as this survey can be carried. Three hundred years

had gone by since the discovery of America, and in the great changes of that period oceanic enterprise had been a causative agent at least as important as any other. The rate of change, slow at first, had steadily increased, but it was still in reasonable proportion to the duration of man's life and the capacity of his mind. Since then the rate has quickened out of proportion to that factor fixed by Nature. Man now is born in one world and dies in another, alien altogether to the world of his formative years. It is stimulating if unhealthy, and where it will lead, none knows. But for good or ill it is the process of modern history.

INDEX